WATERLOO

A PICTORIAL HISTORY

by
Margaret Corwin
and
Helen Hoy

QUEST PUBLISHING/ROCK ISLAND, ILLINOIS

WATERLOO

A PICTORIAL HISTORY

by **Margaret Corwin** and **Helen Hoy**

A limited edition
of 1900
of which this is
Number 1028

This book is the personal property of:

The William Stevenson Family

First Edition 1983

Published by
Quest Publishing
Rock Island, Illinois 61201

Printed by
Bawden Printing, Inc.
Eldridge, Iowa

ISBN 0-940286-02-5

This book is dedicated to Waterloo's
pioneers of the past, the workers
of the present and the city
builders of tomorrow.

TABLE OF CONTENTS

FOREWORD

As one views modern day Waterloo with its ribbons of steel and concrete and handsome, contemporary structures, it is difficult to imagine the lonely, virgin prairie first inhabited by the early setters. Yet, it was the dreams and hard, honest toil of the pioneer that carved a town out of the wilderness and laid a solid foundation for future Waterloo prosperity and growth.

Complementing the drive and determination of the pioneer was the public-spirited entrepreneur adding his piece of the dream to put Waterloo in the forefront; building the bridges, mills, railroads and factories transforming the frontier town and agricultural community into a farm implement manufacturing mecca. Whereas many settlements and towns in the new west died, Waterloo flourished.

Through Civil War, floods, fires, fevers, the Great Depression, two World Wars, Waterloo grew, sometimes slow and steady, sometimes in fevered haste.

Today, Waterloo is a thriving metropolitan area, well-known for its productivity and renowned for its "army of workers." Its churches, schools, parks, cultural facilities, professional and social services lend quality and texture to a first class city bordering the Cedar River.

Life has been good in Waterloo and the future, with all of our resources and history of accomplishments, looks bright.

But while Waterloo citizens ought to be concerned about the future, they should not fail to look back to the dreamers and workers of the past. Knowing the strength of our community's roots binds us to an even greater confidence in the stability of our future.

Within the pages of *Waterloo: A Pictorial History,* the city comes alive through photographs which serve as open windows to the past. These mini time capsules freeze the personalities, events and landmarks of preceding generations. Well documented by local authors Helen Hoy and Margaret Corwin, this edition enables us to share in the excitement and vitality of a city on the grow.

It is our hope that this handsomely illustrated volume will prove a cherished addition to your family library and a valuable collector's item as the years go by.

In 1845, at age 24, Mary Melrose Hanna, "The Mother of Waterloo," first set foot on the site of present day Waterloo. The clear beauty of the Cedar River, the rippling waves of blue-joint prairie grass and the rich loam inspired the petite woman to declare, "Oh, I did not think there was such a place this side of heaven."

Her six-foot husband, George Washington Hanna, observed that the river would provide water power, the graceful timber line, needed fuel and shelter and the virgin prairie soil would be their sustenance.

The decision made, Mary Hanna looked across the river to the bluffs sprinkled with oak and maple and made her prophetic statement to her two young sons, "This seems to me to be the river of life and over yonder is Canaan. Let's cross over. Boys, if you live long enough, you will see a fine town grow up on those hills."

Earlier in the spring, Mary, her husband, their two children, John Quincy and James Monroe, along with Mary's brother, John Melrose, had left White county in eastern Illinois in an ox-drawn wagon. They crossed the Mississippi at Rock Island and followed the Indian trail between Moscow and Nashua, branching off to reach the Cedar River.

According to Mary's diary, they arrived at 11 A.M., July 18, 1845.

After the Black Hawk Purchase opened up the great northwest, the Hannas were part of the flow of adventurous homesteaders who, with a vision and courage to match, left the security of east coast settlements and launched out into the great unknown where civilization was not encroaching on their doorstep.

They had heard about the Cedar Valley, the richest part of Iowa, and they were coming to stake their claim.

While Hanna and Melrose walked in opposite directions up and downstream looking for settlers they had been told were in the area, Mary dispatched her two sons with fishing poles to catch supper. It is reported they caught nineteen rock bass and watched an elk, two deer and a buffalo drink at the water's edge.

Having found no one, the men returned. They missed meeting William Sturgis, founder of Cedar Falls, who, because of family illness had returned for a few months to Iowa City.

Next morning, in accordance with Mary's wishes, the family forded the river at a place above the rapids with a solid rock bottom (presently below Park Avenue and the Railroad Bridge). They drove their team of oxen up the slope, following the old trail across Black Hawk Creek. A mile further, on a ridge half in timber and half on the prairie, the highest point between Waterloo and Cedar Falls overlooking the entire valley, they selected a spot to build their home.

In the afternoon, while the men again scouted, a party of 200 Sioux, reputedly the fiercest of the local tribes, camped on the river flats. Mary, afraid that the Indians would steal her boys, guarded over them and their covered wagon. After gawking a while, the Indians returned to their camp.

In the meantime, the men had found a hump-backed trapper named Dyer who invited them to share his shelter, a crude pen built of poles. During the night, gunshots alarmed Dyer who suspected the Indians were warning the settlers to move on.

Early next morning, in beginning fulfillment of Mary Hanna's prophecy and dream, the men began to cut down and hew out some rough timber to construct their 18x24-foot log cabin.

With the first blow of the axe, on July 19, 1845, a city was born.

Photo Courtesy of Waterloo Public Library

CHAPTER I

The
Early Years

One hundred and thirty-eight years ago, after a wearying five hundred mile trek, George and Mary Hanna arrived at the present day site of the city of Waterloo. The crystal clear stream, the tall blue-joint prairie grass waving like "dark green foam on a light green sea" so charmed Mary Melrose Hanna that she would not be moved from this idyllic spot.

The Hannas were not the first so mesmerized by the beauty of the Cedar Valley. In 1837, a Frenchman, Gervais Paul Somaneaux, a trapper for the American Fur Company was the first recorded white man to make a semblance of settling in what became Black Hawk County. After passing a tranquil summer in the area, he abandoned his temporary quarters to return north.

The Sac and Fox Indians had first laid claim to the rich valley before the advent of the white man.

Around 1825, big business was transacted in the area when St. Louis traders came to barter flour, guns, traps, mirrors, blankets, tobacco, "fire water" and colored calico for the squaws in exchange for the Indian furs, venison, smoked buffalo meat and maple sugar.

In the 1830s, French loggers from St. Louis came to plunder the large groves of cedar, rafting the timber downriver where the durable and fragrant wood drew good prices as trim and finish lumber in lavish homes in bustling St. Louis.

The Black Hawk Purchase opened up the land west of the Mississippi and by the mid-1840s, the Indians had ceded Iowa to the U.S. government and pushed westward one step ahead of "the paleface."

Within a few years of the Hannas' arrival, a stream of settlers followed, drawn by the promise and challenge of the fertile plains. With prairie schooners loaded down with plow, tools, bedding and buffalo robes, they came to a land "where the breaking of bread was as important as the breaking of sod."

Five years after Mary Hanna prophesied the town's birth and future prosperity, the 1850 Black Hawk County population stood at 135 residents augmented by 100 cows, 40 sheep and 183 hogs. The enterprising pioneers had, in that same year, produced over 2,000 bushels of corn and 3,300 pounds of maple sugar. All of the hardships borne, the frigid winters, isolation, sickness and lurking animals washed away before the sound of the prairie lark, the smell of the mellow loam, the green carpeted prairie untrodden by the foot of man.

If farmers and townsmen were not trying to shoot pesky wolves and coyotes, they went to the woods to augment the daily fare with deer, quail, elk and prairie fowl. In the spring, the hunter and farmer could watch thousands of birds and prairie fowl take off in flight, the whirring of their wings like the sound of distant thunder and their mass almost darkening the sky.

In his 1929 article, "When Waterloo was Young," Roger Leavitt, son of the prominent banker John H. Leavitt, claims that George Hanna said they chose the name Waterloo because they expected a great victory over Cedar Falls in the county seat fight. The historic courthouse battle was truly a civil war in miniature.

The pioneers were, after all, "hard-headed, forceful men, many of them coming here on foot or in covered wagons with no money but plenty of determination to succeed. They were men of deep feeling." And when their ire or passion was raised as it was over the courthouse prize, with its promise of future prosperity and prestige, they would fight as hard as they could fell tracts of timber — vigorously. When Waterloo had won the courthouse, Cedar Falls residents swore they would never again set foot in that "upstart" Waterloo. After a few years, relenting, how sheepishly they passed their fellow townsfolk on Waterloo byways.

Similar pride and passions were aroused between east and west Waterloo as the two went eyeball to eyeball not only over the courthouse but over every principal and prestigious edifice erected over the next five decades.

The saw and flour mills that sprang up on both sides of the river were harbingers of prosperity and attracted more homesteaders. Real estate prices soared from the $1.25 originally paid per acre to $25 and as high as $200 for choice commercial lots.

When the pioneers arrived, the only way to cross the Cedar were the fords at Fourth and Tenth Street, that is, until Samuel Lanfear May established his ferry business. The first bridge was built in 1859 after the devastating 1858 floodwaters had everyone navigating the downtown business area in boats. The same floodwaters heralded the arrival of the *Black Hawk* paddlewheeler that had the townsmen envisioning grandiose but short-lived dreams of trade with Europe and the wide world beyond.

In the early days, Waterloo was a frontier town extending three-quarters of a mile up and down both sides of the river and six blocks out in each direction with South Street and rustling prairie grass marking the boundary.

Most of the settlers were poor, honest folk living in log cabins with tree trunk steps and whitewashed walls. Rain and sleet seeped in along with a host of moths, flies and mosquitoes. The pioneers' greatest blessing was his spirit of independence and ingenuity and the faith that he could triumph over the toughest trials and somehow manage to "pull on through."

Before the Civil War broke out, there were many "silver tongued" orators standing on the steps of the old Congregational Church on Fifth and Jefferson decrying the evils of slavery and applauding John Brown while the townfolk passed around copies of *Uncle Tom's Cabin*.

When John Hanna asked his mother if he could enlist, Mary Hanna's reply was characteristic, "Go, my son," she said, "Go. If I did not have any sons to send, I would enlist myself. I could at least carry water to the soldiers on the field and help care for the dead and dying."

Some of the pioneers' grandfathers had fought in the Revolutionary War and their desire to preserve the Union at all costs was fierce. Many boys from Waterloo and the county marched off "shouldering their muskets, returning with an empty sleeve or not returning at all." Every loss of life was the valley's loss, every victory was jointly celebrated and every defeat mourned by all.

In the four day interim between the news of Lee's surrender and Lincoln's death, the populace plunged from supreme elation to abject despair. The settler had always identified with the homespun wisdom of "honest Abe" who, like them, had been a pioneer, ploughed, planted, split rails and loved the smell of the virgin soil and moist timber.

Young Roger Leavitt, son of the Honorable John Leavitt watched, in great consternation, as his "stern, self-controlled Puritan" father threw himself down on the bed and burst into tears when he learned of Lincoln's assassination. That night, in front of the Iowa Central Hotel, Waterloo citizens sank to their knees to pray for their country. Without Lincoln, they did not believe the country could "pull on through."

When peace came over the land, tens of thousands of young men were discharged in the west. They swelled the ranks of western settlers coming to the choice land of the Cedar Valley as farmers, tradesmen or to help the railroads continue their westward expansion.

Two weeks before Fort Sumter had been bombarded in March of 1861, the first Dubuque and Sioux City train had chugged into Waterloo, heralding another milestone in the city's history. After the war, other trunk lines made their debut, laying down track into Waterloo. The town was booming: marketing agricultural wealth in the east and securing supplies by rail in return, eliminating the time consuming labor of teaming in goods from Dubuque and Cedar Rapids.

Cedar Falls and Waterloo again drew swords over which town would be accorded Illinois Central division point status and win the prize of housing the I. C. machine shops. Cedar Falls, as the end point of the terminus, felt confident they would be chosen. But, in 1865, when railroad building had resumed and it became necessary to shut the water off the Cedar Falls' mill race so a bridge could be erected, the two Cedar Falls mills, the largest and perhaps the greediest in Iowa, made the mistake of asking $300 a day compensation from the Illinois Central. Some local historians believe this arrogance turned the heads of the railroad's top brass in the direction of Waterloo who, by contrast, had plied the company with gifts of money and land.

In 1865, with the population gaining on 3,000, Waterloo still resembled a western outpost. The streets were lined with hitching posts and, on market days, crowded with farmer's teams and lumber wagons loaded with wheat. In winter, hogs were dressed and brought to town to sell or ship, further congesting the horse and wagon traffic.

The downtown business landmarks of those early days included Forry's and Snowden drug stores, Raymond Brothers general store, Thunnisen's Bakery and Robinson's leather and fur goods which shared space with Rensselaer Russell's grocery business. After the Civil War, the store sold vintage army blue overcoats with capes which were worn by every well-dressed farmer. Ice cream was five cents a dish at Sindlinger's next to the Iowa Central House whose grand opening was celebrated in 1864 as the dancing and dining highlight of the social season.

There were "57 varieties of sidewalks" back in those days, rough platforms of varied height, size and material, to challenge even the most agile pedestrian. Well worn paths marked the residential area along with "cow pies." Lanterns came in very handy for romantic couples indulging in a late night stroll.

The popular general store sold calico, candy, dried herring, coffee, tea, hooped skirts, crackers by the barrel, dried fruit, brown sugar in barrels and hogsheads and, in winter, fresh oysters for the oyster suppers that went so well with social singsongs and winter sleigh fests.

In 1869, Waterloo was the site of the full eclipse of the sun with many scientists converging on the town from across the nation to watch "the rare and beautiful sight."

There were schools on both sides of the river since the early 1850s as the pioneers valued education. By 1867, 900 children were enrolled in public school. Many children of prominent citizens attended Miss Anna and Elizabeth Fields' seminary, originally for young ladies of promise but later opening its doors to the male presence. The rural children who boarded carried in a week's supply of food on Sunday nights: twisted fried cakes, fresh sausage, cornbread and dried applesauce to eat and share with their roommates.

In the summertime, when school was out, the young people swam and boated on the river and in the creek.

They played tag, post office, pull-a-way and challenged one another walking on stilts with some of the neighborhood girls putting the boys to shame.

Winter was fun for everyone. Sledding, skating and a sleigh ride "with your best girl tucked in at your side under a warm fur robe with a hot soapstone to keep your feet warm. You had a good excuse for holding hands. Then, instead of a balky gas engine, imagine a spirited horse with bells a jingling as you drive to a neighborhood town on a bright, moonlight night over crisp snow sparkling as if covered with diamonds. Then the hot oyster stew and the ride home again! Oh, boy, those were the days."

The pioneers were tireless workers but certainly knew how to enjoy life as well. There are many generations but only one is afforded the honor of being called pioneers. The Hannas, Mullans and Virdens, the first pioneer families, were men and women "cast in steel" who laid a sound foundation upon which future generations of Waterloo citizens could productively build.

This early Waterloo map prepared by John Hartman, a former publisher of the *Waterloo Courier*, shows the locations of two old Sauk and Fox villages. Excavations reveal an Upper Village (present Cattle Congress grounds and McElroy Auditorium) and a smaller, Lower Village at the John Deere Component Works.

The x's and +'s on the map, scattered over a three mile radius, indicate existing and obliterated Indian burial mounds. East Waterloo's first settler, James Virden, in 1849, was witness to a mound building after an Indian battle. The warrior was placed in a sitting position on the ground, a blanket around him, his gun crossing his knees. Around the body, his cohorts built a small palisade of hickory slabs, to keep wild animals at bay, and, finally, dirt was thrown over top until a large mound was raised.

Map Courtesy of Helen Hoy

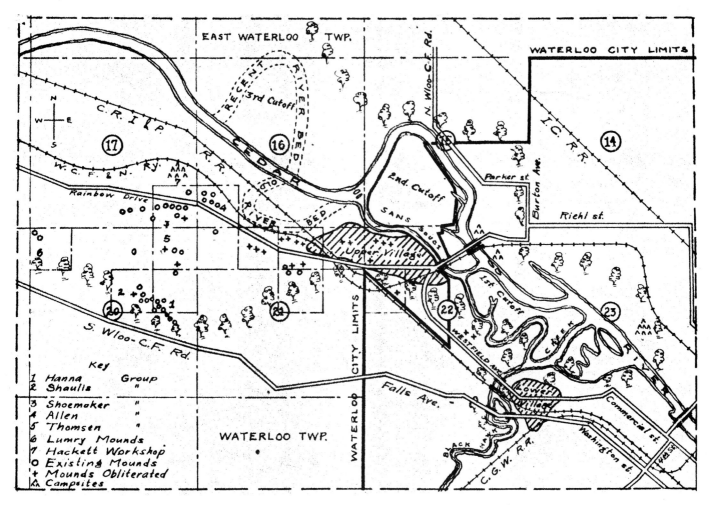

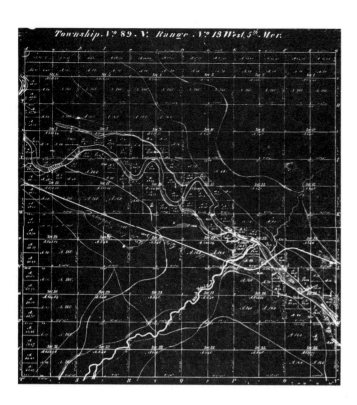

This original survey plat of Waterloo Township showing streams, timber and trails was officially filed in 1846, one year after the Hanna's arrival and the year Iowa became the 29th star on the Union flag. The deputy surveyor was E. L. Haven. One side of a square represents 40 chains or half a mile. The Cedar River is the meandering lines that snake from top left of the map to the lower right. The river has since been straightened at many points. Black Hawk Creek cuts up from lower left to join the Red Cedar. The trail lines were nothing but well-beaten paths in the grass made by the Indians who always traveled single file, in the open, for fear of ambush. With the advent of the white man, the trails became wagon roads and, in the course of time and progress, the super highways and roads of today.

Photo from Crossroads on the Cedar

THE PLACID CEDAR

"Mosk-wah" meaning "red", "wak-wah", for "cedar" is the name the Indians gave to this placid river in honor of the many juniper trees along its riverbanks.

The Indians, Sauks, Fox (Mesquakies) and Winnebagoes found an ideal place to fish, hunt, hold pow-wows and later trading sessions with the "paleface" in an area called Turkey Foot Forks, seven miles north of Cedar Falls, at the confluence of three rivers; the Red Cedar (Cedar River), the West Fork of the Cedar and the Shell Rock (the three resembling a crude drawing of the toes of a wild turkey).

Photo Courtesy of Leonard Katoski, Glimpses of Waterloo

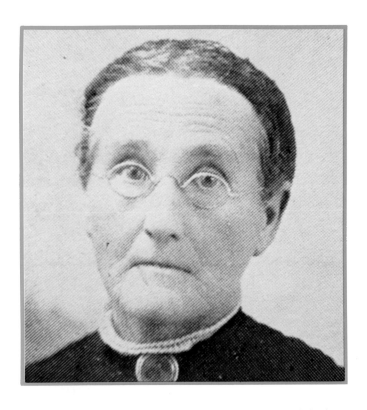

This quartet of stalwart pioneers represents the first and third families to settle in Waterloo (Prairie Rapids Crossing). The second settler, William Virden Jr., died during the Civil War and no photo of him is available.

Mary Melrose Hanna (top left) was born in Edwards County in 1821 and died on November 12, 1912, appropriately as the oldest resident of Black Hawk County. She married George Hanna in 1837, at age 16, and came to Waterloo eight years later. They had 8 children, one of which, James Monroe, died shortly after arriving at the new homestead. Their son, Philip, gained distinction as consul to Venezuela and Puerto Rico. The Hanna pioneer cabin served as community center, church and courthouse for the nascent community.

George Hanna, (top right) born in White County, Illinois,1817, died in Waterloo in 1890, having served as both Chaplain and Justice of the Peace. Known for his generosity in donating land for the town's first dam, mill and schoolhouse, he was not only Waterloo's first settler but also the original town booster.

Charles Mullan, (bottom left) the enterprising third settler, was born in 1811 in Lycoming County, Tennessee, moving to Morgan County, Illinois before coming to join his brothers-in-law, William and James Virden at Prairie Rapids in June, 1846. Mullan served as the first postmaster, county surveyor, realtor and businessman extraordinaire. He died in 1874. His wife, America Virden Mullan, (bottom right) was born in Tompkinville, Kentucky, in 1817 and died in Waterloo in 1902. Her parents moved to Wayne County when she was eight and she married Charles in 1842. The mother of seven children, America drew the respect and friendship of both pioneer and Indian brave alike.

Photos from Hartman History

On June 1, 1846, 23-year-old James Virden walked 100 miles from Dubuque, via Delhi and Independence, to join his brother, William Virden Jr. and his brother-in-law, Charles Mullan, at Prairie Rapids (Waterloo). His parents, William and Martha Virden Sr., pioneers of Kentucky and Illinois, had passed on their pioneering spirit to their numerous offspring including William Jr., the first settler to join the Hannas in 1845 and James himself who gained recognition as East Waterloo's first settler. The three pioneer families who settled Waterloo were all inter-related; America Mullan was a Virden and William Virden Jr., who had travelled part of the way to "the promised land" with the Hannas had married a sister of John Melrose and Mary Melrose Hanna.

It is interesting to note that the average age of the original three pioneer families of Waterloo, upon arrival, was 26 and, at the time of their death was 80.3, verifying the description of one early county historian who referred to them as men and women "cast in steel."

Photo from Hartman History

This "sturdy frontiersman" was, along with the Hannas, one of the first Waterloo settlers. Born in Edwards County, Illinois, March 21, 1818, John Melrose possessed the trusting, generous character of the early Waterloo pioneer: leaving his store to help a fellow settler bring in the harvest or selling goods on credit even to settlers passing through to another location. He rested solely on a promise or note to repay when fortunes improved. In 1864, while assisting a sheriff and poorly armed posse apprehend some horse thieves, Melrose was shot in the back of the neck, the bullet exiting below his ear. A man of tough mettle, he recovered. He eventually relocated in Wright County, married and when his first wife died, like other settlers of the time, was quick to remarry. He fathered three sons and died on March 31, 1884.

Photo from Hartman History

This is typical of the first cabins built here by the settlers. According to Mary Hanna's diary, her cabin would have looked much like this one. This is the way she described her home.

"We selected our claim and built our cabin of logs and covered it with clapboards. We had one six-light window (six panes, probably bought in Dubuque) and one door. We cut hay, put it down and covered it with carpet, which was all the floor we had until cold weather; then we split logs and made what was called a puncheon floor (logs laid evenly in dirt). Our furniture consisted of a table and stools made of split logs. We brought two chairs with us. Our bedsteads had one leg and were made of poles put into holes in the logs of the house."

The bedstead Mary Hanna speaks of was ropes pulled tightly together supported by sticks or poles drilled into the wall. The doors had no lock and easy access was gained by simply pulling on the leather latch string.

Photo from Hartman History

This is an 1846 drawing by America Mullan of her cabin, probably sketched for the benefit of relatives back east. The humble abode was the site of the first Waterloo church service when missionary Methodist, Ashbury Collins, came riding through in 1847. A less welcome visitor appeared one day when America was alone and Charles Mullan was away surveying. An Indian entered her pioneer cabin, poured out a few gold pieces, indicating he wanted "the little white papoose", America's baby, Lizzie. When America refused, the brave stalked sullenly away. The Indians sometimes came begging for settler food which usually consisted of beans, corn bread and pork augmented by wild game, deer, buffalo, wild turkey or smoked or fried prairie chicken. Wild strawberries, grapes and hazel nuts were also plentiful in season. Beaver, mink and otter provided warm, winter furs.

Photo Courtesy of Helen Hoy

As farmers, early settlers planted flax the first year, followed by corn, wheat, cane and buckwheat. Farming was primitive as seed corn was dropped laboriously by hand, covered with hoes and cultivated with a shovel plow. Hay was cut with scythes, gathered into windrows with rakes and forks. The small grain was cut with cradles, raked and bound in sheaves by hand.

By night, prairie wolves and coyotes made the most hideous and terrifying howls. More terrifying by day was the occasional roaring prairie fire set by the Indians.

Dry goods and finished lumber had to be hauled from Dubuque or a three day run into Cedar Rapids. The nearest mail pick-up was in Marion. Mirey sloughs sometimes had both wagon and settler "neck deep" in mud.

Yet, to make up for the toil, drudgery and loneliness, there was the pioneer spirit that was to build the great state of Iowa, of neighbor helping neighbor, cabin and husking bees, not to mention the matchless Indian summers and sunset over the verdant land.

Photo Courtesy of Waterloo Courier.

The fireplace was the focal point of the pioneer cabin used for heat, light and cooking. This elaborate reconstructed model, housed in the Grout Museum, shows the four-foot backlog with wide swinging crane holding the iron kettles. Several different fires from hot burning to slow were required to make a meal of prairie chicken stew and dumplings, venison rump and baked apples with maple syrup. The fireplace was built from field or glacial stone and mortar made from limestone burned in a kiln. Swallows flying above the chimney would send feathery contributions into the room. Small wonder that the pioneer woman's number one request, after the sale of the first wheat crop in Dubuque, would be for a four-legged stove with elevated oven.

Photo Courtesy of the Grout Museum

Waterloo Winter Scene Circa 1860 at Park and Commercial. "Were it not for the cold winters, it (Waterloo) would doubtless have been selected for the Garden of Eden." So wrote one lonely bachelor to his girlfriend, Mathilda, with "600 miles intervening between thee and me." Despite attacks of fever, ague or scarlet fever, there was skating on the river (frozen over to a depth of three feet) and ice fishing of pike and pickerel and sledding parties to the Big Woods or to visit friends in a time when New England style hospitality abounded and "there was no wide gap between cabin and castle." So severe were the winters of '56 and '59 that frozen heads of stock were seen in every barnyard and pallbearers left coffins on top of a snowbank till spring. Not all homes were frame as pictured above, but many were crudely built with cracks and crevices. With temperatures, a frigid 40 below, it was not uncommon to hear a settler say, "I dug through a bank of snow to get from my bed to the stove this morning."

Photo from Hartman History

This 1853 view shows a total of 15 homes in West Waterloo with a county population of 135. The Mullans' cabin is upper center and the Hannas', who had moved in from the farm "to help the village along" is in center left. When Mullan filed application for a post office, he filled in the name Waterloo. One account says he selected the name from a U.S. post office guide while another gives credit for the name to Mary Hanna who saw resemblance between a photo of the famous Belgian town and the view from her cabin window. Nevertheless, on December 29, 1851, under U.S. President Fillmore, Waterloo had a post office box on the Mullan's front porch in America's old teapot. In the photo, you see Samuel May's ferry hauling a team and covered wagon across at a charge of .50¢, (footman 5¢ and free on the Sabbath and election day). 1853 saw the county's first "most spontaneous and spirited Fourth of July" celebrating 77 years of freedom. With fife and drum, they made "the woods ring with music while singing 'My Country 'Tis of Thee,'" after which Sheriff John Virden read the Declaration of Independence. They ran foot races, roasted a pig, baked pies and cooked "everything cookable in the county."

Photo from Crossroads on the Cedar

Nelson Fancher, an ex-California gold miner, opened Waterloo's first general store in 1853 when he took his "fine span of bay horses, Dick and Ned" to Dubuque and loaded up on dry goods, ready-made clothing and farm implements which sold like "hot cakes." He also provided occasion for one of the town's early marriages to Elizabeth Virden. (The first nuptials performed by Justice of the Peace, George Hanna, were in 1851 between James Virden, Elizabeth's brother, and Charlotte Pratt, the vivacious, comely daughter of Judge Pratt.) The Fancher wedding was the social event of the season with a huge pyramid pound cake two feet high gracing a table in front of a fireplace filled with crabapple blossoms. Mrs. Virden used 25 pounds of butter in baking pies and cakes for the occasion. The couple, who also farmed and were grain dealers, built a 32 x 40 two story home with walnut siding and three fireplaces which was home to every itinerant Methodist preacher in a 100 mile radius.

Photo from Hartman History

The original plat of Waterloo showing claims on both sides of the river was filed on June 24, 1854 and extended from Eleventh to Mullan Street and Franklin to South Street, representing approximately 1 1/2 square miles. The following year, Judge Pratt, James Virden's father-in-law and principal owner of east side properties, died, and the sale of his 119 lots totalled $115,000, causing a real estate and building boom in the town. As the town grew, there were many firsts. Doctor McKinley, the first doctor (who played a fine fiddle) came in 1853. The first lawyer, John Randall, came a year later and was elected county judge. One of the first tragedies was the death of two-year-old Mary Virden, daughter of William Jr. and Rebecca, in 1848, when her clothes accidentally caught fire.

Drawing from Crossroads on the Cedar

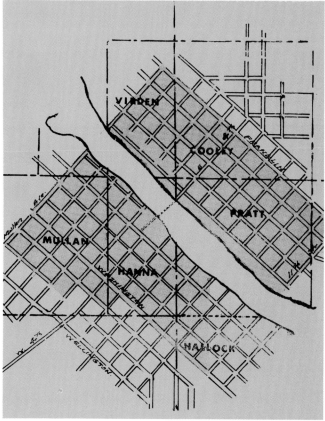

The first schoolhouse, a 16 x 22-foot log building, erected in 1853, doubled as a church with services equally divided between Methodists, Presbyterians and Baptists. The credit for the first Waterloo church goes to the Presbyterians. Completed in 1856, one year later, in the face of the '57, financial crisis, it was sold to the Baptists to become the First Baptist Church (photo). The first school taught on the east side was in Myron Smith's home and was taught by Mr. O Hardy (who, by the way, caught the worst of the pelted egg yolks in the infamous Cedar Falls/Waterloo courthouse skirmish.) The first hotel on the west riverbank was built by Seth Lake and sold to Henry Sherman whose enterprising wife opened the first ladies' bonnet shop. The hotel had 16 beds with prairie hay ticks in a single dormitory room, umbrellas to keep out the rain and sleet and a cow bell to alert the proprietor.

Photo from Hartman History

The Early Settlers Association had their first meeting in Washington Park, in 1884, with "Squire" Hanna and Charles Mullan as guest speakers. George Miller, an early land surveyor, was named president, J. H. Leavitt, the promiment Waterloo banker, treasurer and James Virden served on the first Board of Directors. Pioneers who had settled in the county before 1855 assembled for a group photo. One of the first members of the organization to die, in 1886, was 93-year-old Mrs. Martha Virden, mother of William Jr., James, Isaac, John, Oscar and sister, Elizabeth Virden Fancher.

Photo from Black Hawk County Atlas

During the 1858 high waters, the ferryboat twice broke its cable and went over the dam. The need for a bridge spanning the Cedar was imminent. The person of Judge Couch inspired confidence as he led the subscription drive for bridge funds and was himself the largest subscriber at $1,500 out of the total $4,000. (His mill during the flood, cut off from the east side business, had suffered disastrously.) Along with the lumber firm of Beck and Nauman, Couch served as contractor. The subscriptions were mostly paid off in work, with every able-bodied man cutting up timber donated from Charles Mullan's Sans Souci island and rafting them down to build the piers made of unsawed logs built into a crib and filled with stone. The first Waterloo bridge was completed after the summer of 1859. Although the townspeople favored a Fifth Street Bridge, Couch, as principal financier had it built across from East Fourth Street so wagons could pull right up in front of his mill.

Photo Courtesy of Don Durchenwald

In 1858, floodwater brought not only tragedy but the hope of triumph. On October 5, 1858, a little paddle steamer, the *Black Hawk,* braving the treacherous shoals of the Upper Cedar reached Waterloo. A wildly enthusiastic group of Waterloo businessmen, dreaming of direct trade with Europe not to mention reduced freight shipment of goods, gave a magnificent banquet for the Cedar Rapids captain, J. J. Snouffer and crew, with flags unfurled and numerous toasts glorifying Waterloo's navigational future. Not to be outdone, a Cedar Falls contingent, led by the merchant, Andrew Mullarkey, asked the captain to bunt against the Waterloo dam so Cedar Falls could stand at the head of navigation. On the sideline, Waterloo's John Brooks, on a soapbox, warned the Cedar Falls boys that if they tried to tear out the Waterloo dam now or before the *Black Hawk's* return trip, "to bring their coffins if they wanted a decent burial". The *Black Hawk* did make a run at the dam but because of the current could not reach it and a dejected Cedar Falls contingent returned home.

Drawing Courtesy of Helen Hoy

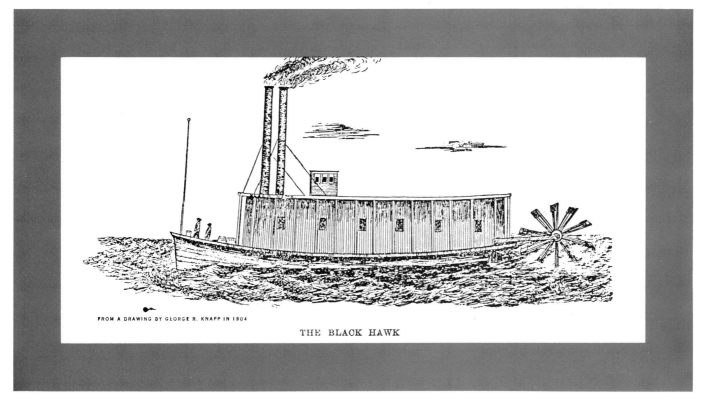

FROM A DRAWING BY GEORGE R. KNAPP IN 1904

THE BLACK HAWK

The first brick edifice built in Waterloo on Commercial near Fifth Street housed the courthouse records wrestled from Cedar Falls in 1855 until 1857 when the courthouse was built on the east side. Judge Hubbard, the owner and resident, had established a store on the ground floor. The courtroom was located upstairs doubling as a Masonic and Oddfellows Hall. The multi-purpose building also served as the Waterloo post office of 1855 for which Judge Hubbard, originally a Connecticut blueblood, received $50.55 "compensation" for that year.

Photo Courtesy of Leonard Katoski

Since Cedar Falls had its own saw and flour mill, Waterloo was not to be outdone. In April of 1854, one week after the town plat was filed, George Hanna, James Virden and Charles Mullan contracted with James Eggers of Fulton County, Illinois, to build a log and brush dam across the Cedar for power purposes, as well as a sawmill in return for Mill Square property (from Commercial to the river between Park Avenue and Fifth Street) and other lots in lieu of payment from the three promoters. Two months later, Eggers had raised the water level two feet and had a sawmill rolling which, unfortunately, had slow and outmoded equipment. Eggers sold his property for $4,000 and left town.

Pictured below is the supplanting dam built in 1856 almost on top of the original one.

Photo Courtesy of Don Durchenwald

The pioneer families were supplanted by city builders and none was more prominent than Judge G. W. Couch. A P. Hosford and Edmund Miller, capitalizing on the land and timber boom, had opened up the first bank in 1854 and along with the Elwell brothers purchased title to James Egger's Mill Square. They commissioned G. W. Couch to modernize and take over Egger's sawmill, raise the water level to five feet by means of a timber crib and rock fill dam, build a mill race and build a flour mill. This Couch accomplished in 1856. What a blessing for the townspeople not to have to make a tiring trip to other towns just to grind flour. Competing mills soon sprang up. In a single year, the population trebled and streets were lined with teams bringing logs and grain to the mills.

Photo Courtesy of Clarence Baldwin

Judge Couch erected a big frame dam just below the old brush and log dam in 1864. Four years later, he built the City Flour Mill (pictured above in foreground) which was destroyed by fire in 1900. A woolen mill was built after the Civil War giving local impetus to sheep farming. Across the river, on East Fourth Street, (present National Bank location), is the Cedar Mill, a five story stone building built by a fine miller, Miles Spafford, who was killed when some heavy mill machinery he was hauling tipped over and crushed him to death. A group of citizens, including Nelson Fancher, completed the mill building and incorporated under the name Cedar Mill Company. (Beat'em All Barbed Wire, written on the woolen mill, was one of the companies that used the building after the woolen mill failed).

Photo Courtesy of Clarence Baldwin

"Revolutionary warfare" erupted between Cedar Falls and Waterloo, making lifelong enemies, over the location of the county courthouse. In 1853, Black Hawk County was authorized to set up its own government, no longer under the jurisdiction of Buchanan County. Country records went to the larger and already platted Cedar Falls in a "two-by-four" room over Mullarkey's Store. Waterloo threw down the gauntlet, when on their 1854 plat, they designated present Lincoln Park as "Courthouse Square." A group of "spirited" Waterloo citizens invaded Cedar Falls to steal the county records but were driven back by an egg wielding Cedar Falls faction. A county vote on January 19, 1855, voted 388-260 in favor of the more centrally located "up-start" Waterloo. Temporary quarters were J. C. Hubbards' brick store, the only one in town, on Commercial Street, while east and west now vied for the courthouse. Another county election, with Cedar Falls voting against the west side, located the new structure between 9th and 10th on the east bank. The new courthouse costing $27,000 was dedicated May 4, 1857, with bells ringing in the rotunda.

Photo from Hartman History

There was a lot of excitement in the Waterloo of 1856 with the mills and the many strangers from New York and the east coming into town to invest in land and timber tracts. John H. Leavitt, a Massachusetts born civil engineer, first hitchhiked a ride into town with Nelson Fancher and his team of spanking bay horses, and after surveying portions of Black Hawk County, worked for the newly opened Hosford and Miller bank on the second floor of the Sherman House on Commercial. Two years later, the 25-year-old Leavitt opened up his own bank (photo) across the street and met with "instant success."

Photo Courtesy of Waterloo Public Library

On Monday, July 19, 1858, the town's first major tragedy occurred when two young girls, Melissa Corson and Ellen Case drowned near Lover's Island when their boat capsized after hitting an unseen snag. William Fiske, who was rowing, held on to a tree limb and was saved but went insane when learning of the girls' fate. The name Lover's Island derived from a legend that a misanthropic Easterner, living alone in the area, shot his foot while hunting and would have died had not an Indian girl found him and nursed him back to health. They fell in love but her Indian chief father forbade the match. They met secretly on this island of tall elms until some braves were sent to kill the white man. Seeing their intent, the maiden sacrificed herself by taking the arrow designed for her lover. They both died. Lover's Island washed away in the 1884 flood.
Photo Courtesy of Don Durchenwald

John H. Leavitt was president for 50 years of what later came to be called the Leavitt & Johnson Bank and in that interim was one of the pillars of the community. With four other citizens, he founded the First Congregational Church and for fifty years served as trustee chairman and was one of its most faithful members. In 1870 and '71, he was elected to serve in the State Senate. He was chairman of the committee which brought the Illinois Central machine shops in 1869 from Dubuque to Waterloo as well as chairing the committee which secured the Chicago Great Western Railway for the city.
Photo from Hartman History

In 1858, William Hartman set up a creaky Washington handpress at 613 Commercial and published the *Black Hawk Courier*, changing the name to the *Courier* in 1860. Before 1890, the *Courier* would move 11 times, up and down many a flight of stairs and surviving on "faith and cornmeal" along with the bushels of wheat and firewood that patrons brought in, in lieu of the $2 annual subscription payment. When frigid temperatures froze up the office equipment, the paper was skipped with profuse apologies emanating from Hartman in the following edition. The weekly paper consisted of business card advertisements, poetical readings and general news. In the photo, the "exclusive" Raymond Brothers General Store was located below this early *Courier* location.
Photo Courtesy of Clarence Baldwin

Couch's wooden bridge was carried downstream in an 1866 flood and replaced with a second timber structure partially (and sparsely) funded by the County Board of Supervisors which had supplanted the county judge system of government. Increased heavy wagon traffic demanded an iron bridge so after a second bitter battle with the County Board, most of which were rural members, $14,000 was allocated towards what ended up being an expensive $28,000, 600-foot bridge built by the Ohio Bridge Company in 1872. The bow type iron truss bridge, nevertheless, served well for 30 years. Note the caution sign above the entrance, "Do not run. Do not drive at a pace faster than a walk." It also clarifies the number of livestock and how far spaced apart, a farmer could drive over the bridge at any one time. 1. City Flour Mill; 2. Woolen Mill; 3. Couch's original floor mill; 4. Sawmill.
Photo Courtesy of Clarence Baldwin

The Iowa Central Hotel was the renovated Sherman House where many a newly arrived settler laid his weary head. Henry Sherman had built a 1½ story, 25x50-foot addition to a log cabin tavern he had purchased from Solomon Ayers. The upper half of the "hotel" was called "The School Section" with cots numbered 1-16. When a patron asked for a single room, Sherman, candle in hand, led him to an upstairs cot and when the patron queried, "Is this a single room?", Sherman countered, "Do you see more than one room up here?" In 1864, the highlight of the social season was the grand opening of the 3-story, 50-room Iowa Central House. Partygoers danced away the Fourth of July night while owners showed off the spacious dining room, billiard parlor and barbershop. The hotel's register contained the names of notable lecturers like Harriet Beecher Stowe, author of *Uncle Tom's Cabin.*
Photo Courtesy of Don Durchenwald

Iron linked Iowa with the east in 1856 when the first engine puffed across the Mississippi from Rock Island to Davenport. The Dubuque and Pacific Railroad was organized to build an iron road westward across Iowa through to Sioux City and eventually to the Pacific. The Dubuque and Sioux City reached Dyersville in 1857; Independence in 1859. The world-shaking event happened when the Dubuque and Sioux City rolled into Waterloo at 5:05 P.M., March 11, 1861, one week after Lincoln's inauguration. The crowd, gone mad in cheering, later toasted the arrival of the first iron horse across the prairie as "the chain that unites us all". (The American Standard engine pictured, 4-4-0 (four pilot wheels, 4 driver and no trailing wheels) was typical of the 1860s.)

Photo Courtesy of Don Durchenwald

Secession, abolition and John Brown had long been the topic of conversation over stake and rider fences but when, in April of '61, the South bombarded Fort Sumter, Waterloo (and the Union) was shocked. Five thousand Cedar Valley residents turned out to wave and kiss good-bye 100 county volunteers getting on a Dubuque and Sioux City train commandeered by a Union general. Twenty-year-old Lorraine Washburn (photo), son of pioneer, Levi Washburn, and a private in the Third Iowa Infantry, was the first Waterloo soldier killed at Blue Mills Landing, Missouri. When the train brought Peter Dorlan, the first wounded man home on a cot, businesses were closed and the plow left, to welcome the hero home. For the next four years, the town waited for the train to bring news of Bull Run, Shiloh, Gettysburg, Vicksburg . . . and the lists of dead and wounded. The night Waterloo learned Lee had surrendered, April 11, 1864, Commercial Street became a mass of humanity with the Central House lit from top to bottom, cannons firing, rockets flying, a torchlight parade eight abreast led by Judge Couch and J. H. Leavitt singing "The Battle Hymn of the Republic".

Photo from Hartman History

The Burlington, Cedar Rapids and Northern (later part of the
Rock Island) ran its first train into Waterloo station in 1870. When
the city's third line, the Chicago Great Western reached Waterloo,
it built stations on each side of the river. The other two lines who
had, heretofore, located their passenger depots far from the town
centre, followed their competition's example and built stations
downtown. This station at Bluff and Fourth was built around 1890.
The transportation advantages caused many firms such as
Litchfield Manufacturing, Jerald Sulky Company and Rath Packing
to relocate in Waterloo. By 1915, 75 trains a day moved in and
out of the Waterloo-Cedar Falls area and along with the electric
Waterloo, Cedar Falls and Northern, carried 70,000 cars of freight
annually.
Photo Courtesy of Robert Levis

The Waterloo I. C. roundhouse, in the zenith of the steam era, was a bustling place where engines were routinely greased and oiled or placed in storage. More extensive repairs were done in the neighboring shops.

By 1900, the Illinois Central, valuing Waterloo as their most important division point on the lines between Omaha and Chicago, spent $700,000 expanding and rebuilding the yards and shops as well as building new division offices using land donated by the community. In the busy years, the yards employed as many as 1,500 men, making the railroad the city's biggest employer.

Photo Courtesy of Robert Levis

Cedar Falls, as terminus of the railroad, naturally expected to house the machine and repair shops of the Illinois Central who took over the Dubuque and Sioux City line in 1867. On November 12, 1870, the I. C. shops were moved from Dubuque to Waterloo leaving rival city, still smarting from the courthouse loss, accusing her neighbor of underhanded dealings. While the Illinois Central was debating between the two cities for their shops, a Waterloo committee chaired by the shrewd and Honorable State Senator, John Leavitt, helped settle the question by giving the company $23,000 in cash and 70 acres of choice land within the city limits. (East Waterloo, now with courthouse and railroad, was in its glory.) Initially, the buildings consisted of a roundhouse with 14 stalls, (on right in photo) machine, blacksmith, carpenter and paint shops, all brick and fireproof. The yards employed 160 men who could service 38 engines.

Photo Courtesy of Robert Levis

The volunteer fire departments, with their parade uniforms and fire fighting bravado, added a swashbuckling romance to the era. When wooden businesses were crowding Commercial and Bridge Streets, a group of Waterloo businessmen, on May 25, 1861, organized Hook and Ladder Company No. 1. The forty volunteers sporting red shirts, black belts and glazed silk caps were ready for the Fourth of July parade. The bucket brigade, in 1864, progressed by adding an old Red Jacket engine found buried under rubbish in a Chicago station. Waterloo bought its first steam engine, the Jeanie Jewel in 1879. This photo shows the Red Jacket Fire Department and Waterloo Band on the southwest side of Commercial with Snowden's Drug Store on the left next to the Leavitt Bank.

Photo Courtesy of Don Durchenwald

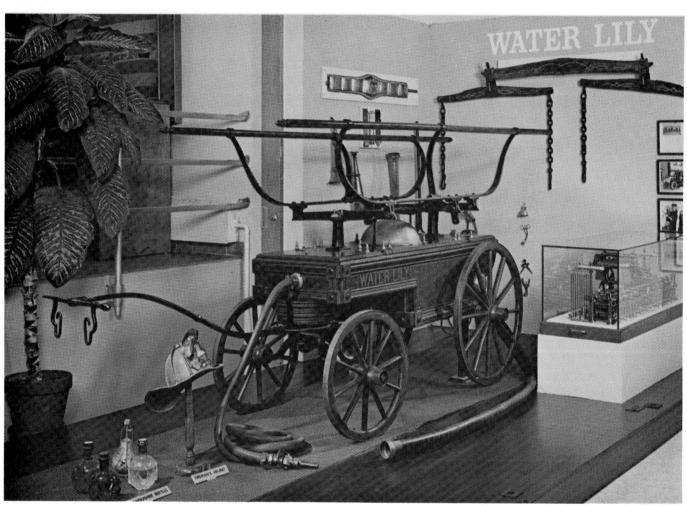

In 1871, 18-year-old Clarence Hollister constructed a hand fire engine, the "Water Lily" (photo) which could throw a horizontal stream 100 feet in the air. A company of cadets averaging 12 years of age, was organized to man the new engine. In 1871, the city also built its first engine house and purchased a Water Witch hand engine for $800 from Janesville, Wisconsin. Water Witch Engine and Hose Company No. 2 was formed and, as Cedar Falls was without a single engine, their first challenge was saving the Overman Block. The Water Witch, loaded on an Illinois Central car, made the trip to Cedar Falls in a record breaking eight minutes!

Photo Courtesy of the Grout Museum

Henry Nauman, a man of indefatigable energy, Waterloo's first manufacturer, came to the town in 1856, and hauled all the material used in building his home from Dubuque. In the ensuing years, Nauman was a leading spirit in many of the town's early enterprises. His partner, George Beck, a German immigrant whose father built the first U. S. canal on the James River in Virginia, also came to Waterloo in 1856. After working in the boot and shoe business and involved in mills, he opened Beck and Nauman's, dealers in all kinds of pine lumber, lath, shingles, sashes and doors. Fortunately for the two pioneer manufacturers, the profits from the sash and door business kept the wolf away from the door of their woolen mill which failed in 1875 at a loss one source quotes at $65,000.

Photo from Hartman History

Beck and Nauman's (photo), Waterloo's first manufacturing company, met the town's need for a planing mill and sash and door factory. George Beck, in 1866, was named fire chief and, ironically, his first fire was his own, the Beck and Nauman mill which burned at a loss of $12,000. Plagued by fire, the company was, in 1884, to lose a furniture store and warehouse and in 1898, the entire manufacturing plant burned at a loss of $40,000 with only $18,000 insured. Undaunted, the company rebuilt and expanded under Nauman's sons, C. H. and G. W. The Nauman company covered one square block at Cedar Street and Park Avenue and also manufactured drug, bank and store furnishings. In front of Beck and Nauman's in the picture, you see the mill race bridge built by Judge Couch in 1867 to supply power to the Beck and Nauman woolen mill.

Photo Courtesy of Leonard Katoski

With Waterloo's increase in population and the general growth of all businesses, both industrial and commercial, Waterloo banks acted as pillars of the community working toward "a bigger, brighter, better and busier Waterloo."

The oldest national bank in Waterloo was the First National, organized in 1865, and it came to be one of the strongest in the state with such eminent Board of Director members as J. W. Rath and H. W. Grout. The First National built a two story edifice at the corner of Fourth and Sycamore.

In the momentary flurry of 1907 which compelled the banks of nearly all cities of the entire country to go "upon the paper basis," the First National along with other Waterloo banks still paid out in coin and currency, a sign of strength and stability. With their high capitalization, Waterloo banks outranked similar sized cities such as Cedar Rapids and Dubuque.

Photo Courtesy of Leonard Katoski

The First National Bank had an impressive first floor lobby to complement its reputation "as the Rock of Gibraltar" in the banking business. Which it was for many years. However, during the Great Depression, when a multitude of banks failed, the First National also succombed.

Photo Courtesy of Don Durchenwald

When the plat of Waterloo was filed in 1854, one block on each side of the river was designated for a public square. The east side plot became Lincoln Park (right photo) and the west one, Washington (top photo). Ideal locations, they were both equidistant from the river on Main Street. The owners of the respective blocks, Mullan and B. M. Cooley, retained the original titles. When the courthouse battle erupted with Cedar Falls, Charles and America Mullan, owners of the west side square property, deeded the land for a courthouse site to the legislature which promptly returned the block, refusing to be pressed or influenced. On March 1, 1864, the Mullans deeded the block for $450.00, "to the people of Waterloo for a public square and pleasure ground." The square was named Washington Park in 1872. Lincoln Park was purchased from J. L. Cooley, brother of B. M., for $1,000, in 1902. It has been beautified since this 1898 photo.

Photo of Washington Park from Waterloo: The Factory City of Iowa
Lincoln Park Photo Courtesy of Leonard Katoski

In 1868, Waterloo, all of three square miles and 4,000 inhabitants, took a giant progressive stride and voted to incorporate. The new boundaries reached as far as Newell Street, Linden Avenue, Williston and Belmont, an irregular shape drawn to follow areas of settlement. It wasn't until Waterloo's 50th anniversary, population 16,000, that the citizens climbed the steps of city hall and voted 662-233 to extend into "Greater Waterloo," sixteen square miles, with the western line of the new city limits three miles short of the eastern Cedar Falls boundary. Shortly thereafter, almost two square miles was lost when some rural Waterloo plaintiffs complained that the city was digging into farm territory that was neither ripe for the picking or the platting.

Photo from Hartman History

Waterloo's location, water power, agricultural output, combined with superb rail facilities made things hum in the Waterloo of 1865.

This is what Commercial Street looked like in 1865, from the present Waterloo Courier building, at the place where West Fourth jogged to make room for the mills. Across the corner you see the Raymond Brothers store, pioneer merchants since 1855, and the Union Gallery Building, where Conway Square stands today. Across the street from Raymond Brothers stands the little stone structure known as Benight's Building and hall, next to the Robinson Brother's Leather store, a three story building owned by Rensselaer Russell and the newly remodeled Iowa Central Hotel (present Holiday Inn) where Lee's surrendar was so joyously celebrated. Note the wooden sidewalks, hitching posts and plentiful parking space.

Photo Courtesy of Waterloo Courier

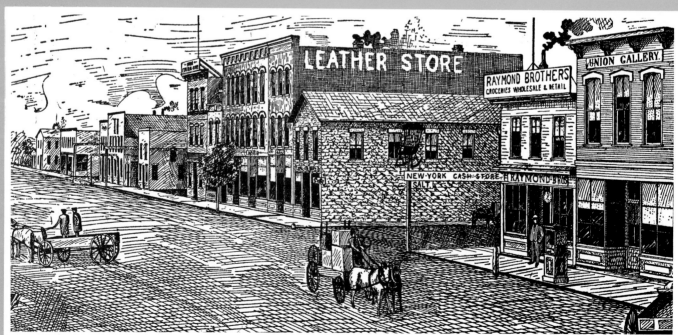

This schoolhouse was built in 1858 on a half acre of ground, a mile from town, and was purchased by the county for $10.00. Henry Grout, as State Senator and "public-spirited" citizen, for whom Grout Museum was named, was a student here. His sister, Frances, for whom the Grout School was named, also attended. In 1880, the school was abandoned and became a residence. Later it became the Church of Latter Day Saints, then was sold to the Four Square Gospel Church. In 1961, a new building was built on the site and the school became a church educational building. The pioneer stonemasons laid the 2-foot thick walls in a rubble-work style, using stones of irregular sizes and shapes. Of all the early schools built in Waterloo, this one rural school, now in an urban location, is the only survivor.

Photo Courtesy of Waterloo Public Library

This sleeply looking scene is an 1870 view of the northwest corner of East Fourth Street between Water and Sycamore. In 1875, the Waterloo population (5,500) and agricultural production had leveled off. Looking to infuse fresh blood, the city fathers made every effort to draw new factories but many, such as the broken-down St. Louis stove factory and a harvester works, failed miserably along with the woolen mill. There was, notwithstanding, steady business and population growth. In retrospect, this trial and error period was merely priming the pump for the future growth, in the late 1890s, of Waterloo as a major midwest industrial stronghold.

Photo Courtesy of Don Durchenwald

The sign of the big gold watch at the corner of Commercial and Bridge (West Fourth Street) in 1880 meant Joe's Plunder Store with offices of Dr. G. G. Bickley, upstairs. The Irving Hotel later occupied the Bickley Block site, followed by the Montgomery Ward building, presently owned by the *Waterloo Courier*. "Plunder Joe" knew both how to advertise and the value of a catchy trade name.

Photo Courtesy of Clarence Baldwin

Like other pioneer businessmen, Rensselaer Russell, who lent his name and money to the Russell-Lamson Hotel, had his fingers in several entrepreneurial pies. Initially, in 1857, he started up his own banking business along with an M. H. Moore. When the First National Bank opened in 1865, he transferred his banking interests over and went full time into real estate, buying and selling a lot of land throughout Grundy and Black Hawk County. In 1860, he raised the Russell Building, the town's first three story multi-purpose edifice, used for business, concerts, social and religious functions. The last 10 years of Russell's life were dedicated to looking after his extensive real estate interests. His first daughter, Genevieve, died at age six but his second daughter, Lillian, took care not to marry until after her father's decease. In 1896, she married Clyde Lamson, builder of the Russell-Lamson Hotel in 1914.

Photo from Hartman History

Rensselaer Russell, a "genial man of sterling qualities" was born in New York state, in 1828, one of ten children and son of an immigrant English carpenter. He was head salesman of a dry goods store before bringing his wife, Caroline and young daughter, Genevieve, to Waterloo, in 1857 in his wagon. The Rensselaer Russell home, a lovely brick structure, in the Victorian Italianate style, located on the corner of West Third and South Street, is one of the oldest homes still standing in Black Hawk County. It was built by the successful realtor at a cost of $6,000 in 1861. Mr. Russell, at age 33, also purchased the entire square block naming it Russell Square. Many Fourth of July picnics and celebrations were held on the spacious lawns. No one has ever lived in the home except descendants of the Russell family.

Photo Courtesy of Leonard Katoski

In the early days, it was reported that Miles Spafford, the miller, was the only local resident to sport a top buggy; everyone else made do with a board nailed across a wagon. In the ensuing decades, however, fashionable landaus and broughams graced the thoroughfares such as these pictured on Jefferson Street. Of a Sunday, the gay blades of Waterloo would escort a prospective bride around town in a conveyance rented from a livery. Klinefelter's Livery, in later years, offered 15 such classy conveyances for hire.

Photos Courtesy of Helen and Jean Klinefelter

The West Side School at West Sixth and Washington was considered one of the best in the state when it was completed in late 1869. A scant six months later, it was consumed by fire. The loss was set at $30,000 with insurance covering only $10,000. Classes were held in a church and offices in the Nauman Block until a second school was built. Note the cow grazing. In the early days, cows roamed at will until Mrs. John Leavitt, disapproving of "cows at large in town," headed a petition drive to get the critters off the street.

Photo from Hartman History

CHAPTER II

1875-1905

The scene had changed considerably from the hot summer's day in 1845 when the Hanna's white-topped prairie schooner crested the west side embankment of the Cedar River. Between 1875 and 1910, log cabins gave way to stately residences, the general store laden with flies and fur pelts was razed to make room for impressive business blocks. Ten miles of asphalt and paved brick formed broad avenues lit by 536 gas lamps: a great improvement over muddy, darkened roads and paths. Electric streetcars replaced the horse drawn ones and the Waterloo Cedar Falls and Northern meant rapid urban and interurban transportation interlocking into a network of trunk railroads with tentacles reaching into the four corners of the nation.

There were three daily newspapers, three weekly and three monthly. City parks and concert halls were a boon to the naturalist and the aesthete.

Circuit riding preachers visiting bi-weekly on horseback to baptize in homes or solemnize wedding vows were replaced by pastors and priests assigned to churches built by growing congregations.

Pioneers coming in wagon trains, on foot and by stage coach turned into an influx of immigrants arriving by rail, seeking an opportunity to worship freely, to put their hand to the plow or help build the infant industries.

In the area of communications, Miss Anna Speicher of Iowa Bell Telephone was Waterloo's first "Hello Girl" in 1883. Waterloo was one of the first cities in the midwest to have its own telephone exchange serving 30 subscribers at a charge of $5.00 per month. For a long time, Iowa's Governor Horace Boies of Waterloo had number one as his personal telephone listing.

In the realm of education, the class of 1876, two girls and a boy, comprised the first class to graduate from the West Side High School; whereas, East High produced their first graduates, two young ladies one year later.

Up until 1884, there were two beautiful islands, popular picnic and trysting places in the middle of the Cedar River. One smaller one stood where the first pier of the Fifth Street Bridge now stands on the west side out in the river; the

other larger Lover's Island, 500 feet by 150 was located near the east bank from Sixth to Eighth Streets. Gradually, floods reduced their size and the great flood of 1884 washed them away, trees and all.

The volunteer fire departments purchased their Jeanie Jewel steam fire engine in 1879. By the end of the era, both east and west sides had fine fire stations and a paid fire and police department, the latter east and west combined force consisting of eight officers. Sad to say, this progressive era saw the area's first violent crimes. In 1877, one Jacob Gomeringer crushed his wife's skull with an axe and committed suicide a few days later. By 1879, over the span of the year, 122 prisoners had been incarcerated, the majority non-violent malefactors, and 11 of these convicts had escaped.

Besides enduring two severe blizzards in the 1880s, Waterloo citizens of this period were subjected to a strange "epizootic" epidemic affecting most of the horses during a single winter. The horses were stable ridden and local oxen were employed to pull the town bus.

According to the 1875 census, Waterloo had a population of 5,500. The 1870s had been solid, steady building years spearheaded by the locating of the Illinois Central shops in Waterloo and followed by the coming of the Chicago Great Western and the Burlington, Cedar Falls and Northern railroads. The number of small shops, artisans, blacksmiths, livery stables and commercial outlets continued to grow.

Names like Mullan, Hanna and Couch were supplanted by other "public-spirited" men including H. B. Allen, Matt Parrott, Horace Boies, Judge Bagg, the Cascadens, father and son, F. E. Cutler and the incomparable William Galloway. Old names like Leavitt, Beck and Nauman, Russell, Fowler, Snowden and Wangler continued to be a power in city building.

By 1880, there were a total of 25 factories and business was up almost 50% over the previous year. If Waterloo was going to continue to grow and prosper, the city fathers concurred that Waterloo must make the transition from an agricultural town to a city of factories and manufacturing. After a frustrating trial and error period, the city caught the spirit of factory building and never once looked back.

One industry followed in the wake of another. Having the means of employment attracted a larger work force to Waterloo. Rath's came in 1891. Between 1890 and 1900, the population doubled from 6,000 to 12,000. Better stocked stores like Black's encouraged patrons from outlying districts to come in and trade, affording opportunity for greater employment.

Wholesaling grew apace with Waterloo merchants reaching out to serve a goodly portion of Iowa as well surrounding states.

As the principal interior city of the northern half of Iowa, there was pride in Waterloo's churches, schools, history of accomplishments. On both sides of the river, the slogan promulgated by the Commercial Club and Board of Trade, "Waterloo Way Wins" was on everyone's lips.

In 1900, Waterloo was the fastest growing city in the Midwest. New civic buildings, a Y.M.C.A., a courthouse, two new libraries, a federal building, touched off ferocious warfare between east and west requiring delicate negotiation to balance one edifice on one side with one of equal value on the other.

Waterloo had its own famous race track at the turn of the century, the half mile Home Park Race Track built by one of the best trainers and race track builders in the country, C. A. Niles. On July 4, 1899, a capacity crowd of 2,500 packed the grandstand, leaned over the railing and cheered as they witnessed a record for the fastest mile trotted in Iowa. Auto races (5 miles in 10 minutes) were added in 1902.

In 1904, in a rare moment of unity, east and west joined hands to celebrate Waterloo's semicentennial patting each other on the back for their fast-paced growth into one of the premier manufacturing centers of Iowa. The secrets of success in their rise to prominence were location, transportation, strong local banks and an enterprising work force.

In 1905, Waterloo was known as "The City of One Hundred Smokestacks" with its 100 manufacturers and jobbing institutions doing an annual business of eight million and boasting the largest flouring mills in the state. Waterloo was well on its way to prominence as an agricultural and farm machinery manufacturer producing anything from manure spreaders and horse collars to buckwheat flour and Waterloo frankfurters. The pump was being primed for the next stage of phenomenal growth.

Pride was evident in the 1910 promotional booklet, *Waterloo, The Factory City of Iowa* which stated: "Waterloo is rapidly becoming one of the great factory cities of the west. The smoke stacks of industrial activities are becoming more and more numerous every year. Smoke stacks are the fore-runners of prosperity. Smoke stacks of industry create the army of workers. Smoke stacks bring population. Population creates necessity for new and enlarging commercial activities. Smoke stacks make possible the maintenance of the homes and families of industrial workers and they in turn make possible the growth and stability of mercantile, financial and commercial pursuits of every kind and character.

The lesson is "Create more smoke stacks of industry."

In the next era, this is precisely what Waterloo did "with tireless energy."

In 1880, the first paving of Waterloo was done on Commercial (photo) and East Fourth when broken rock called macadam named after the inventing British engineer McAdam, was laid with much man and horsepower expended. Up until then, roads were awful-deep in dust in the summer and muddy trails and puddles on the main streets in the spring. Note the piles of bricks lining the sidewalk.

Photo from the Waterloo Public Library Collection

A blizzard struck the northern part of the country on March 14, 1881, hitting Waterloo with four-foot deep snowdrifts seen here piled up along Commercial Street (present site of the Holiday Inn). This blizzard was a whimper by comparison with the blast of '88 when passengers in stage coaches froze to death and farmers were later found a few feet from the barn door. Children, on both sides of the Cedar, remained in school all night and teachers in West Waterloo installed ropes from schoolhouse to grocery store. As the storm raged, temperatures dipped to forty below during the great blizzard of January 4, 1888.

Photo Courtesy of Don Durchenwald

The Irving Hotel, when it opened on June 17, 1884, ranked as one of the foremost hotels in the state and registered 10,000 guests in its first year. Three hundred invited guests attended the opening day festivities of the deluxe establishment, decked out with flowers and Christmas trees. The $5 a plate dinner, reflecting superb culinary artistry, included 13 meat entrees, a selection of ten desserts, not to mention other assorted and tantalizing accompaniments. An Italian band from Dubuque stationed in the lobby entertained the guests at appropriate intervals.
Photo Courtesy of Leonard Katoski

The Irving Hotel, the "Waldorf of Waterloo" in 1884, had a fine lobby where guests and men of leisure could relax, smoke and read the weekly paper. Landlord A. G. Smith charged $2.00 a day — rooms 50¢, 3 meals a day at 50¢ each. The facilities included a basement billiard and pool room along with a four-chair barber shop. The Irving Hotel had some high-powered names as backers: Nauman, Cascaden, Whitney and Daniel. In 1937, the hotel was razed to make room for Montgomery Ward.
Photo Courtesy of Don Durchenwald

In 1914, James Black, the Irishman born in Donegal County, erected a magnificent eight story dry goods store, the pride of East Waterloo. Young James Black had come to the young town in Waterloo in 1892 and in a 20 by 80-foot space on the second floor of Parson's Music Hall, he opened a little "emporium" (photo). The canny merchant, "a big man physically and morally", soon expanded beyond notions and Irish lace and took over the first floor before raising his 1914 140 x 100-foot modern emporium.

Photo Courtesy of Leonard Katoski

Matt Parrott, born a New York "Yankee," was a Waterloo publisher and one of the city's most honored state officials, serving as lieutenant-governor of Iowa in 1895. Originally from a family of ten children, young Matt got printer's ink in his blood at age 13 and in 1854, ended up a full-blown journeyman printer. "On a tramp," he worked for a host of newspapers and publishing houses throughout the Iowa-Illinois region keeping an eye out for opportunity. In 1869, he and J. J. Smart bought the democratic *Iowa State Reporter* from H. Q. Nickelsen, a Waterloo east side paper "breathing its last," which they resuscitated in republican colors adding a bindery and stationers' business. In no time, half the northern portion of the state was using Parrott blank books. Matt Parrott served on the City Council from 1877-'81, was elected Mayor in 1877, re-elected almost unanimously for two more terms, elected state senator by a wide majority, was a candidate for governor in 1897. He died in April, 1900.

Photo Courtesy of Matt Parrott and Sons Printing Company

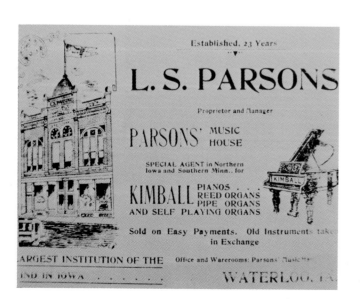

The largest wholesale and retail piano house west of the Mississippi was the L. S. Parson's Music House located on East Fourth Street. Established in 1876 by L. S. Parsons with H. D. Parsons as General Manager, the Music House and its branch agencies placed thousands of pianos and organs in homes throughout Northern Iowa. The upper floor housed the 500-seat Parson's Music Hall catering to concert companies and lectures, and was considered, before the advent of Brown's Opera House, to be the finest concert hall in the state. An ornate grandfather clock from the original building now rests in the home of Virginia Parsons in Waterloo.

Photo Courtesy of Don Durchenwald

48

Barten Crandall

*Mrs. Hoover and Weegei
her Norwegian elkhound*

Lou Henry (Mrs. Herbert Hoover) was born March 29, 1875 in this residence (top left) on the corner of West Fourth and Washington Streets. Her father was a bookkeeper for the First National Bank. Friends and acquaintances remember young Lou as a tomboy who loved to play with horned toads. Nicknamed "Jill", she was one of Waterloo's first feminine cyclists of the late 1880s. A thin and plain young woman, she had a glow and animation which attracted her future Quaker husband, "Bert" whom she met in a geology class at Stanford University. A Catholic priest, in 1899, gave special dispensation for the marriage between the Episcopalian and dedicated Quaker. She made a triumphant return to Waterloo in 1928 as wife of a candidate for the U.S. presidency. Not an Eleanor Roosevelt, Lou Hoover was a capable but unobtrusive first lady. Her love of nature and the outdoors served her well as national president of the Girl Scouts, an organization to which she was devoted. She died of a heart attack on January 7, 1944 in their New York Waldorf Towers apartment after 45 years of marriage to the great humanitarian and elder statesman of the Republican party.

Hoover home photo courtesy of Don Durchenwald
Lou Henry photo courtesy of Roseann Mathews

In the 1880s, the showplace residence of Waterloo belonged to the George Snowden family and was built on land once owned by Rensselaer Russell. Originally hailing from Pittsburgh, Captain George Snowden, in 1865, opened a drug store and stationery business which he operated with great success until 1903. He was recognized as one of the foremost businessmen of the city and prominently identified with projects that aided the development and future of Waterloo. As this beautiful home was hard to heat, the Snowdens were forced to move out every winter. Captain Snowden's family moved to California upon his death and the residence was transferred to Lillian Russell Lamson, daughter of Rensselaer Russell and the wife of Clyde O. Lamson. The Waterloo Women's Club acquired the home for use as a meeting place in 1922 and in 1955 it was almost destroyed by fire. The house is listed on the National Register of Historic Places as a superb example of Victorian Italianate architecture.

Photo Courtesy of A. A. Bengston

In 1891, Henry Besler began work on the brick paving of East Fourth Street. Pavement was laid from the bridge to Franklin Street. The second contract covered the paving of Lafayette Street from Fifth Street to Park Avenue. After the street was leveled with logs pulled by horses, the bricks were transported by wheelbarrow and each brick was laid by hand. By 1912, there was ten miles of brick paving. It was said, that out of town businesses were so impressed with Waterloo's progress in this and other areas, many families and businesses were drawn to relocate in the enterprising community.

Photo from the Waterloo Public Library Collection

The first public transportation system, a narrow gauge horsecar line was constructed in 1885 by the Waterloo Street Railway Company and heralded by much whistle blowing and bell ringing. In the spring of 1886 there were three cars which travelled between the Illinois Central passenger depot and shops at Fourth and Dane Streets and the B.C.R. & N. depot at Mullan and Bluff. The tracks were laid along Fourth Street across the bridge continuing on Fourth Street to Washington Street, to Mullan and across the railroad tracks to the depot. In the winter, cars were put on runners. Drivers, on cold days, tried to be accommodating, going blocks out of their way to give a patron taxi service to their very door. The driver pauses here in front of the Wangler Drug Store on East Fourth and Lafayette.

Photo Courtesy of Robert Levis

An ingenious way to advertise, "North Brothers Tonight" is emblazoned across a horse blanket. This picture was taken in front of Brown's Opera House. The name was changed from Burnham's to Brown's Opera House in honor of Charles F. Brown who, in 1888, remodeled and took over the opera house as manager for the next 18 years. He had shows ranging from classical dramas to trained elephants accompanied by a 10-piece orchestra. Brown's Opera House was destroyed by fire in 1906 in one of the fiercest fires ever to challenge the destruction of the West Waterloo business section.

Photo Courtesy of Helen and Jean Klinefelter

Waterloo was so proud of its opera house, reputedly the finest in Iowa, that the local streetcar company built a loop around the opera house so that every streetcar in the system passed by, one every seven minutes. Originally called Burnham's Opera House, the city's first "class" concert hall was the inspiration of Professor E. W. Burnham who housed his Iowa Conservatory of Music on the second floor. Located at Commercial and Main (Park), on the present site of the IPS Building, the Opera House was dedicated on November 25, 1877. An opening night crowd of 400 patrons at $5 per person, one of the largest assembled audiences in town to date was totally charmed by "a promising American songstress," Miss Emma Abbott and her troop. Scenic artists had been brought in from Chicago to do ceiling frescoes and, that dedication night, 100 kerosene lamps gave off a mellow light highlighting the fresco work and scenery.

Photo Courtesy of Leonard Katoski

The first Lutheran Church was formerly known as the German Evangelical Lutheran Church with a nucleus of worshipers of German descent. (The newly opened land west of the Mississippi had even been well advertised in Europe.) The Lutheran congregation, worshiping in German, first met in 1866 in the basement of the Congregational Church. In 1868, a lot was purchased for $25 at 427 ½ Jefferson (photo). Reverend Westernberger was the first pastor called. The church building was completed in 1872 and was shared with the German Presbyterian (hence the 427 ½ address). Quaker fashion, men and women sat apart, each segregated to one side of the aisle. On October 8, 1906, the Klinefelter-Brown's Opera fire seriously damaged First Lutheran. A new church was raised on Maple and High Streets in 1907 and rebuilt in 1959.

Photo Courtesy of First Lutheran Church

The Cedar River provided ice which was cut in the winter with blunt nosed heavy hand saws as seen in the foreground of this picture. It was then hauled and stored in the buildings visible in the rear. Teams of horses hoisted the ice up the chute using a block and tackle pulley method. Harvesting started when the ice was ten or twelve inches deep, usually in mid January. Ice houses were windowless and immense, with walls about 40 feet high. The walls were double insulated with sawdust. It could be a hazardous business as, on occasion, a horse or workman fell into the icy waters and chattered momentarily until fished out.

Photo from Waterloo Public Library Collection

The impressive building in this artist's sketch housed the Masonic Temple and the important wholesaling institution of Cutler Hardware. The store has the honor of being the oldest in Waterloo. F. E. Cutler established a modest hardware store on East Fifth Street in 1866 known as Weatherwax and Cutler. The business was incorporated in 1891 under Cutler Hardware Company at which time a wholesale section was added. The wholesale business with trade covering Iowa and Minnesota, was so good, in 1901, the retail trade was discontinued. In 1902, their attractive steel and cement four story business block was built at 400 Sycamore. The Canadian born merchant was a member of Waterloo's first city council, an organizer of the Commercial Club and Board of Trade, president of the Humane Society and, a Mason. The Cutler edifice housed a lodge and magnificent banquet room for the Masons. The company was purchased in 1973 by George Clark and Son of Minneapolis. Cutler's inventory was transferred to the parent company in 1975 after urban renewal acquired a three block area of Sycamore for post office relocation.

Photo Courtesy of Leonard Katoski

Founded in Burlington in 1875 by Henry Weis, the Waterloo North Star Company was moved to Waterloo in 1891 and operated at 719 Commercial until 1921 under sole ownership. The box company, making mostly fillers for egg cases, was one of the largest factories of its kind in the west. The fillers were made from strawboard purchased from the sawmills. The collapsible fillers were shipped all over the country. The power for the operation was originally supplied by a fifteen-horsepower gasoline engine. About 1910, electric power was furnished by Citizens Gas and Electric. The North Star finally went out of business.

Photo Courtesy of Leonard Katoski

Conrad Wangler, a pioneer druggist of Waterloo, was a native of Germany, born in Baden in 1851. After crossing the Atlantic alone at age 15, he received his education in Cedar Falls and Waterloo schools before entering the College of Pharmacy at Cincinnati, Ohio. He became a permanant resident of Waterloo in 1878 and, with his brother, R. C., purchased the retail drug business of Carpenter and Smith. Their store was located on East Fourth Street but later relocated to east Fourth and Lafayette (photo). In 1900, the Wangler Drug Company, wholesalers, was organized. By 1903, business had prospered far beyond expectation in the sale of druggists' sundries, drugs, soda fountain specialties, paint and stationer's supplies. A staff of 22 with four traveling salesmen catered to the northern portion of Iowa and southern Minnesota.

Photo Courtesy of Leonard Katoski

"Opportunity tauntingly plays before the dreamer, but succumbs to the efforts of the determined, energetic man" — as it did to Cortlandt F. Fowler, who, in 1870, established the pioneer wholesale grocery business of Fowler Brothers. C. F. Fowler came from New York state to Waterloo on his honeymoon in 1868 at age 23 with his bride and a few barrels of vinegar. In the next 15 years, he, along with brother George, developed their business into one of the leading wholesale grocery houses in Iowa. The company's three story corner brick edifice was raised at East Fourth and Lafayette, adding a four story structure in 1884. The company had its own cheese making factory but bought milk and cream directly from the farmer until 1916. The "father of Waterloo wholesaling" served as director of the Waterloo and Cedar Falls Union Mills, the First National Bank and was a leader in developing Waterloo's excellent park system.

Photo Courtesy of Leonard Katoski

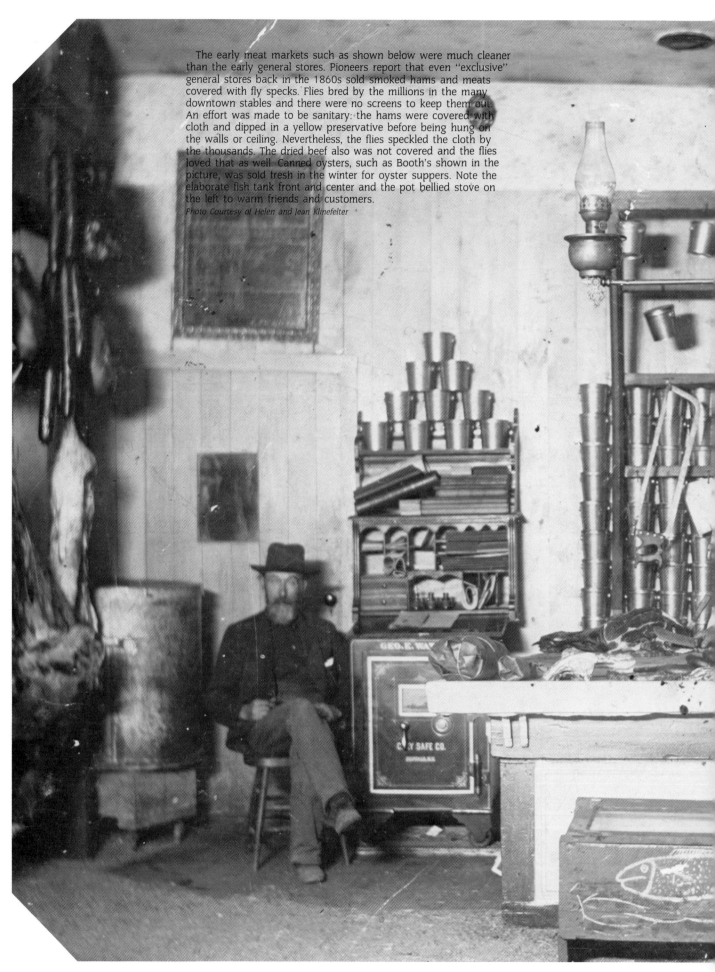

The early meat markets such as shown below were much cleaner than the early general stores. Pioneers report that even "exclusive" general stores back in the 1860s sold smoked hams and meats covered with fly specks. Flies bred by the millions in the many downtown stables and there were no screens to keep them out. An effort was made to be sanitary: the hams were covered with cloth and dipped in a yellow preservative before being hung on the walls or ceiling. Nevertheless, the flies speckled the cloth by the thousands. The dried beef also was not covered and the flies loved that as well. Canned oysters, such as Booth's shown in the picture, was sold fresh in the winter for oyster suppers. Note the elaborate fish tank front and center and the pot bellied stove on the left to warm friends and customers.

Photo Courtesy of Helen and Jean Klinefelter

Waterloo produced an eminent lawyer and statesman, twice elected governor of Iowa, 1890-1894, in the person of Honorable Horace Boies. In 1867, Boies came to Waterloo and entered into law practice with the prominent H. B. Allen under the firm name of Boies and Allen (bottom photo). He was the first Democrat elected governor since 1855 and the fact that he was reelected in a state recognized as a republican stronghold speaks highly of Boies' ability. Henry B. Allen initially opened a law office upon his arrival in Waterloo in 1857 while simultaneously serving as president of the First National Bank. After Allen retired in 1881, the firm became Boies and Couch until Couch was elected to the district court. The building had been clothed in different names over the years but had always remained a law office.

Boies' portrait from Van Metre History

George Lichty came to Waterloo from Pennsylvania in 1870 and went to work as a delivery boy in a grocery store, working up to clerk before opening up his own retail grocery store in 1879. Ten years later, with salesmen from the Fowler Company, E. B. Smith and B. S. Hillman, he organized the Smith, Lichty & Hillman Company, wholesale grocers "with little capital but much pluck." The competition with the Fowler wholesale grocers was positive, adding more volume to the city's business and establishing Waterloo as a wholesale and jobbing center for the Midwest. A new building was erected in 1906 on East Park Avenue with an auxiliary plant facing on Sycamore added in 1910. George Lichty continued as president and, in 1913, became president-elect of the National Wholesale Grocers' Association.

Photo Courtesy of Leonard Katoski

The Waterloo Paper Mill was organized in 1888 and located near the river, east of 18th Street and south of LaPorte Road. A ripple below the Eighteenth Street Bridge is a telltale sign of the remains of a stone dam, erected in the 1880s as the "lower power project". A street named after the mill, "Paper Mill Street" is located in the Rooff Addition. Gladys Street (where the chimney of the old mill stands) was named after John Rooff's wife. The mill produced up to eight tons of strawboard per day (used to manufacture egg case fillers) and employed 75 people. The mill was partially destroyed by fire in 1908 and, it is said, was thereafter used as a "pest" house to isolate those with communicable deseases.

Photo Courtesy of Waterloo Public Library Collection

Newspapers from around the world carried stories of the use of a single granite boulder (photo bottom) used to build the First Presbyterian Church in 1890 at East Park Avenue and Mulberry (above). The boulder, a leftover from a prehistoric glacier, was found on the Henry Grout farm north of Waterloo. This edifice was the third church owned by the First Presbyterian Congregation: they built the very first Waterloo church at Jefferson and Park Avenue in 1856 but because of the financial crisis of 1857 had to sell to the Baptists; the second, a brick church, was built at West Fourth and Jefferson in 1867 and lasted until the "famous Boulder Church" was raised. According to the *Courier*, the 20 x 28 x 32-foot monolith weighed 5,000,000 pounds. Workmen began their labor with "drill, powder and sledge and soon this Napoleon of boulders met its Waterloo". Robert Ripley sent his "Believe It or Not" column around the world on the First Presbyterian Church which has since been torn down.

Photo Courtesy of Leonard Katoski

The trade journals published by Fred L. Kimball broadcast the name "Waterloo" to millions of readers. What was to become the largest dairy publishing house in the world began in 1890 with some borrowed money, two rented rooms on West Fourth and Kimball's vision. *The Creamery Journal* preceded *The Egg Reporter*, started in 1893. In 1895, the company moved into a small printing plant at 187 Bridge Street in the Courier Block. In 1903, Kimball undertook what became "the acme of excellence", *The Dairy Farmer* serving a host of farmers who made their living milking cows and raising dairy cattle. Scarcely had this publication been successfully launched, when Fred Kimball passed away, a year later. The firm incorporated as the Fred L. Kimball Company. In July, 1920, the company erected a new plant at 1900 Westfield Avenue covering 28,000 square feet and employing over 100 workers with branch offices in Chicago, New York, St. Louis and Minneapolis. This view shows part of the staff in 1901 posing in front of the offices on Bridge Street (now West Fourth Street.)

Photo Courtesy of Helen and Jean Klinefelter

Mayor Groat, in 1896, decided that it was high time Waterloo, population 10,000 and "proud of its prospects", should have its own City Hall. The three story building of pressed brick front was completed the same year and housed both fire and police departments, all city offices, east side public library and a one room city jail. Space was rented to organizations on the third floor. In 1911, the chief of police took over this area for his office. It was cooled during the extreme heat by placing large cakes of ice on the basement floor in front of a vent fan which was channelled to the upstairs police quarters. One wall downstairs was used as a backstop for small arms and target range until the stone wall started to crumble. Almost as soon as the building was completed, the city had outgrown it.

Photo from Waterloo Public Library collection

All mustachioed and looking every bit like the Keystone Cops, "Waterloo's own" and entire city police force numbering seven posed, in 1898, for this photo. Mayor James M. Groat, a former Waterloo coal dealer, sits in front. Prior to 1894 there had been a single law enforcer on both the east side and west with one marshall headquartered at City Hall. The trio clocked in from 2:30 P.M. to 4 A.M. working only at night when mischief was brewing. They were, however, like doctors, always on call. One of the police officers' main duties was loading bums onto box cars and hustling them out of town on a rail.

Photo Courtesy of Leonard Katoski

The home of Dr. G. G. Bickley, pioneer physician of Waterloo, was originally built at the corner of West Fourth and Wellington Streets where the Colonial Apartments now stand. After the doctor died in 1911, John G. Miller Sr., the contractor, removed the porches and moved the entire house up West Fourth Street and up the unpaved Kimball Avenue hill (no mean feat) to its present site on Frederick and Kimball as pictured. The edifice, for seven decades, has served as the Miller homestead. Mrs. Frances Miller Clemens is the present owner and resident. Dr. Bickley's son, Dr. G. G. Bickley Jr., continued to serve Waterloo's medical needs after his father's decease.

Photo Courtesy of Leonard Katoski

In 1890, the year that Waterloo's founding father George Hanna died, the *Courier* graduated from a weekly to a daily paper. William Hartman (on the right), leaning confidently against his edifice at 186 West Fourth, surrounded by his staff, looked more the picture of success than in his early years of struggle and poverty. John C. Hartman became editor upon his father's death in 1895, ably assisted by leading stockholder and longtime employee E. Mesick. In 1908, Sinclair Lewis, the author of *Main Street* worked for the *Courier* as a reporter. In the John Hartman era, the *Courier* absorbed competing newspapers, the *Iowa State Reporter* and the *Waterloo Tribune*.

Photo Courtesy of Don Durchenwald

In 1896, the streetcar line was manned by two, a motorman and conductor. The cars started out at 6:20 A.M. and parked in the Dane Street barns at midnight, after each of the three cars had made 18 round trips per day. "Air conditioned cars" were enclosed in winter. Moving east from Elmwood Cemetery, motormen were warned to descend the hill on Fourth Street, which at that time had a steep grade, very cautiously so as not to lose control in case a C.G.W. or B.C.R. and N. train came barrelling through the crossing. In the event a streetcar went dead on the railroad tracks, the passengers were to remove themselves to a safe distance and torpedoes laid on the rail on the engineer's side of the track one quarter mile from either side of the streetcar.

Photo Courtesy of Robert Levis

Louis S. Cass (light suit with tails and straw hat) is seen inspecting the laying of rails of the Waterloo and Cedar Falls Rapid Transit which he established in Waterloo in 1895 when he came to live here. The first streetcar line electrically operated was from Elmwood Cemetery to Cedar River Park, the Chautauqua grounds — a 30 minute run. Eastbound cars (cemetery to park) bore odd numbers and westbound, even. In 1896, Cass, aided by his two brothers, J. F. and S. F., converted (and extended) the horsecar line into an electric one and, the following year, built the line to Cedar Falls. In the next decade, Louis Cass extended interurban tentacles north to Denver and Waverly to connect with the Great Western and, by 1914, had completed an interurban to Cedar Rapids via La Porte, and Urbana. A former Wisconsin lumberman and railroad telegraph operator, Cass, later became chief executive officer of the Chicago Great Western but renounced the position to dedicate himself to the Waterloo Cedar Falls and Northern, successor of the W. and C. F. Rapid Transit.

Photo Courtesy of Robert Levis

A middle-of-the river YMCA to bind together and satisfy the jealousies of both east and west was proposed in 1896. However, it was decided that an island YMCA would mean no basements or baths and the facility would be at the mercy of every flood. The structure, completed in 1898 at a cost of $13,000, was built at West Fourth and Cedar Street. The site was the original Mill Square, where James Eggers built the town's first dam and sawmill in 1854. This new building was a monument to those Christian men who, back on September 28, 1868, launched the association in Waterloo meeting in Dr. Mason's office. A large block of limestone that rolled off the Burlington, Cedar Rapids and Northern provided the cornerstone which was laid on May 16, 1898, proclaimed "YMCA Day".

Photo Courtesy of Leonard Katoski

Charles W. Mullan was six months old when his father, one of the triumvirate founding fathers, came to Waterloo in June, 1846. In 1897, the younger Mullan was elected State Senator of the 38th District, resigning in 1900, the year he was elected Attorney General of Iowa. He served for two consecutive terms. The imposing brick residence, at 516 West First Street, was built by the first generation settler in 1898 and stands a few blocks from the site where his pioneer father built a large frame house. In 1870, Mr. Mullan married Emma L. Hammond, daughter of William Hammond, and they raised four children in this home.

Photo Courtesy of Leonard Katoski

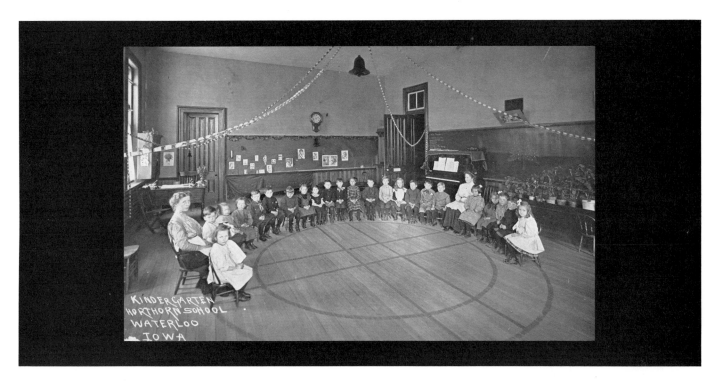

It was at Waterloo's first outdoor street fair in 1898 that the popular slogan "Waterloo Way Wins" was first promulgated. Bands, booths, museums of "antiquities and curiosities" could be found up and down Commercial Street for the three day Peace Jubilee. There was a bowry dance every evening, a midway, "Rough Riders and Bucking Broncos." The motto "Waterloo Way Wins" expressed the city's pride in its rapid growth, achievement and progress over the last decade. "Located in the center of a rich agricultural region . . . the city has become the mecca for man-made implements for farming and dairying."

Photo from Waterloo Public Library Collection

This is the Christmas season as celebrated by the kindergarten class at Hawthorne School. Hawthorne was built in 1897 and burned in September, 1915. There were 23 students in this class, one teacher and a helper, a number and composition similar to our classrooms of the 1980s. In some school areas, because of bad winter weather, school was discontinued over the winter months and resumed from early spring until summer.

Photo Courtesy of Helen and Jean Klinefelter

The Dunsmore House, located at 902 Logan Avenue is one of only two nineteenth century limestone buildings still standing in Waterloo. The other is the old schoolhouse located on Parker Street. The house was built in 1866 by Thomas Chadwick, an Englishman and master stonemason. The rock was brought in from a small quarry near the present Allen Memorial Hospital. In 1873, the home was bought by John Dunsmore, an employee of the Illinois Central Railroad. After his death in 1904, his family left Waterloo and the house remained vacant until 1913 when Fred Michael, the owner of a paint store, purchased the property and completely remodeled and enlarged the home. Dunsmore House was purchased by Louis Townsend in 1926 and by Gwen Garrison in 1968. In 1974, the house and adjoining lot were sold to the Bicentennial Commission of Black Hawk County which took on the job of restoration. In 1983, Dunsmore House was purchased by Antioch Baptist Church.

Photo Courtesy of Helen Hoy

As Waterloo became more prosperous, its citizens took on trappings that reflected the new wealth. People kept fine carriages and horses and even little girls were transported in style such as this graceful landau. Homes, too, became more ornamental with picket fences and green shades lining the residential section. The Ladies' Literary Society had been organized in 1878, a harbinger of the first Waterloo Library. Forty years after its "rough and tough" pioneer beginnings, Waterloo was developing a touch of class.

Photo Courtesy of Helen and Jean Klinefelter

This hall consisted of one billiard table and the rest pool tables. There was no ball return with these tables. The pool sharks you see might be playing pea ball, a popular game of the era. Notice the hall's elaborate metal ceiling and gaslights. The cuspidors (spittoons) lining the floors had to be cleaned and polished every night after the last customer left.

Photo Courtesy of Orville Close

This is the spectacular view of the Union Mill as it burned to the ground on December 29, 1900. It had served the citizens well since the merger, in 1873, of the two larger mills. Then, as now, a big blaze draws a crowd of spectators.
Photo Courtesy of Clarence Baldwin

This picture shows Dr. John O'Keefe, prominent Waterloo physician and surgeon, in his new convertible automobile in which he made house calls. The hood is held down with a strap. The auto is a right-hand drive with the horn on the outside. However, muddy roads and bridge washouts had this and other doctors resorting back to the dependable horse and buggy on many occasions. Dr. O'Keefe, acutely aware that the distance to the nearest hospital in Dubuque, was too far for a population of 13,000, helped, in 1901 to outfit Waterloo's first Emergency Hospital, a 15-bed facility in the old C. A. Smith residence at Seventh and Wellington. Quarters were so tight, instruments had to be sterilized at night in the kitchen after the cook had gone to bed.

Photo Courtesy of the Waterloo Public Library

This marble edifice represents the "great Waterloo compromise of 1900." Because the east side was awarded the courthouse, the west was counterbalanced with the new Post Office-Federal Building. The compromise was effected by Third District Congressman D. B. Henderson, ("The building will go up even if I go down."). The congressman also accomplished the impossible by obtaining $150,000 in federal appropriations which allowed for the extra expense of the marble facade. The building was constructed in 1904 at the corner of Park and Commercial and was used until 1938. The eagle that once graced the building was transplanted to the front of the Waterloo Recreation and Arts Center. The adjacent Knights of Pythias building is now the library's parking lot.

Photo Courtesy of Waterloo Public Library

The Vienna Bakery Company was a business born and bred of meager proportions. After winning out over the "at home" bread baker, the Vienna Bakery became the leading bread company in Waterloo. The factory, located at Mulberry and Elm Streets, was the model of efficiency and order, and was outfitted with the most advanced equipment and ovens. Twenty-five workers were employed and six delivery wagons catered to a large local retail trade and an extensive wholesale business. The Vienna Baking Company was, in 1903, taken over by C. F. Altstadt and W. H. and J. H. Langlas to become the Altstadt and Langlas Bakery.

Photo Courtesy of Robert Levis

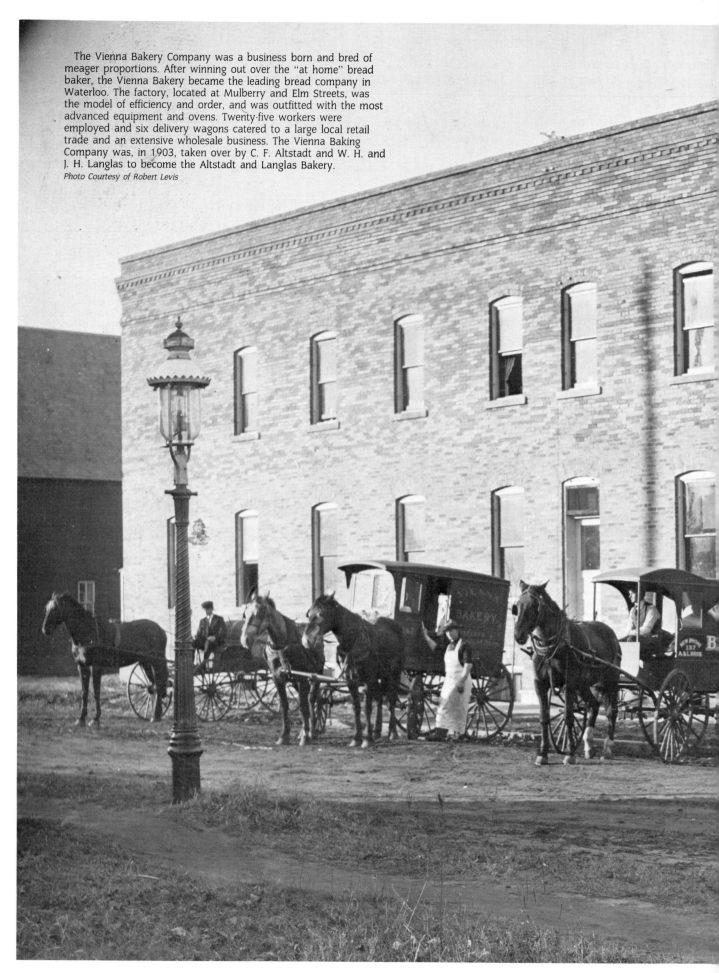

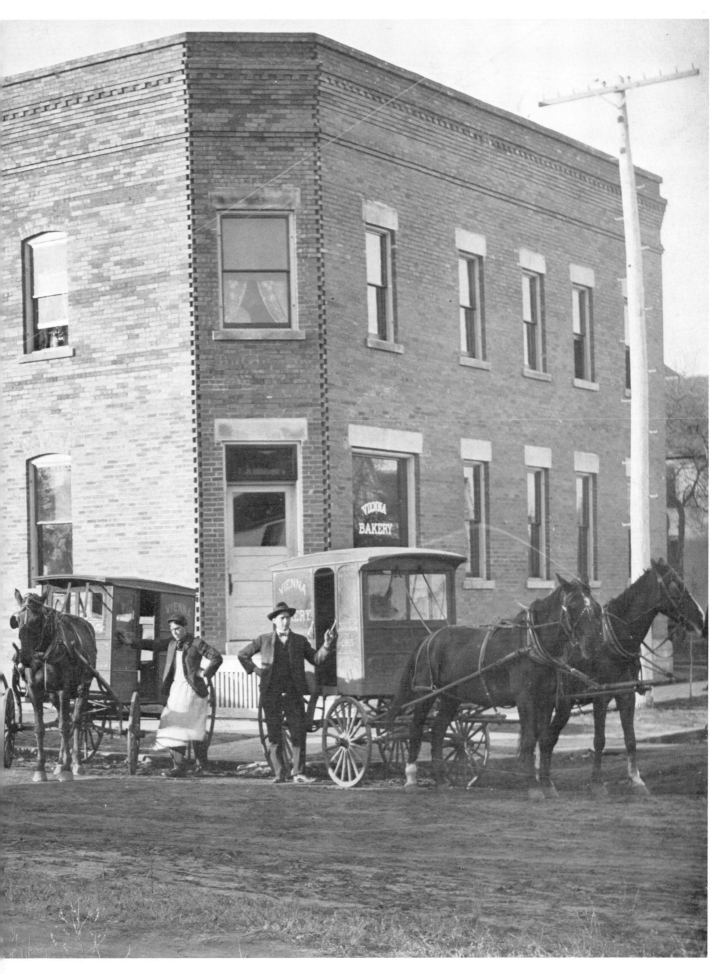

Dry Run was a low watershed originating in the marshes that flooded destructively with every major rainstorm such as on July 3, 1902 when Dry Run ran to a depth of 10 feet within five minutes of a cloudburst. Construction on the new Fourth Street Bridge stopped because the river was rising at the rate of one foot per hour. On July 23rd, the water works whistle shrieked the alarm warning that Dry Run had again become a raging torrent sweeping away sidewalks and bridges. On West Sixth Street, the waters tossed and tore like a tidal wave, sweeping everything in its path. The flood covered 24 square miles and it was this 1902 flood that prompted the Dry Run sewer project. This view looking west down Fifth Street, catches a horse and buggy coming in from Commercial Street. The Commercial House is at the left and the steeple at the right belonged to the Congregational Church.

Photo Courtesy of Waterloo Savings Bank

Photo Courtesy of Don Durchenwald

MENU

****

Oyster Cocktail
Kennedy's Wafers

**

Escalloped Oysters
Celery

**

Cold Roast Turkey   Cranberry Sauce
Mashed Potatoes, brown gravy
French Pea Patties

**

Vienna Bread   Parker House Rolls

**

DRY RUN PUNCH

**

Sliced Cold Tongue   Pressed Veal Loaf

**

Sliced Ham

**

Olives   Radishes

**

FRUIT JELLY

**

Lobster Salad   Waldorf Salad
Wafers   Salted Almonds

**

Ice Cream, La Rose
Devil's Food   Angel Cake
Macaroons   Kisses

**

Pineapple Cheese   Roquefort Cheese
Dent's Water Crackers

Newspaper reporters are credited with suggesting the newly built Dry Run sewer as a banquet hall. So unique was this banquet in a sewer (no rats invited) that newspapers around the world carried the story of the October, 1903 event. In the underground chamber, 450 guests, the women in high heels and richly embroidered gowns, filed down a ready made stairway in a block long section of the sewer between Wellington and Randolph Streets. Many of the guests were representatives of state of Iowa city officials who were holding a convention in Waterloo. Twenty-two feet underground, Mayor P. T. Martin toasted the victory of Dry Run. The $100,000 sewer project constructed by W. Harrabin of Iowa City, provided an underground conduit between marsh and river.

An elaborate menu was featured at the Dry Run sewer banquet. A Dry Run Punch was served, capped off with Roquefort cheese and "water crackers." Fans kept air circulating while Beloit's Orchestra and the Masonic male quartet sent dinner music echoing up the passage. "Golden Rule" Jones, famous reform mayor from Toledo, Ohio, was supposed to have spoken but illness kept him away. F. R. Conaway of Des Moines filled in and praised Waterloo "whose factory whistles can be heard all over the state." The planners of the banquet were plainly astounded by their success and before the decorations were taken down, the ladies of the Progressive Brethren Church held a 25¢ supper in the cavern feeding 500 and turning away 1000! The unique event prompted a Washington D.C. dentist, a Toledo employment agency and a Chicago architect to express their desires to bring their businesses to Waterloo.

Banquet menu Courtesy of Waterloo Public Library

Dapper and dynamic, "Will" Galloway, Waterloo industrialist and developer, held the spotlight during the city's period of rapid and exciting growth. Born in Berlin, Iowa in 1877, Galloway came to Waterloo in 1901 and started a small implement manufacturing plant, eventually expanding into one of the most important manufacturers of central Iowa. He organized the Galloway Gibson Investment Company which developed principal additions such as Prospect Hills, Cedar Heights and Galloway. With his brother, James, he started the Galloway Brothers Company handling farm and flower seeds and buying Canadian prairie acreage to produce oat seeds. Defaulted payments caused Galloway's bankruptcy after WW1 but from Saskatchewan came oat seeds, his salvation, and he was able to buy back the home he had lost and start all over again.

Photo Courtesy of Ross Galloway

William Galloway credited Thomas Cascaden with initiating the industrial development of Waterloo. Thomas Cascaden, was the city's leading industrialist operating a factory at 801 Commercial that manufactured gasoline engines, feed mills and farm implements since 1896. In 1910, the Cascaden Manufacturing Company, founded by Thomas Cascaden, Sr. and operated by Thomas Cascaden, Jr. was purchased by Galloway and merged with the Wm. Galloway Company. The photo shows the Thomas Cascaden, Sr. home (right) which, with turret and opulent woodwork, was typical of the elaborate workmanship in the era when lumber, lumber barons and their salesmen abounded. His son, Thomas Jr., built the home on the left.

Photo Courtesy of Leonard Katoski

The Waterloo Bottling Works used the following as their advertisement in the early 1900s. "WATERLOO BOTTLING WORKS. EVERYTHING THE BEST. THE BEST OF EVERYTHING. THERE ARE OTHERS BUT NONE SO GOOD. We not only guarantee our goods to comply with the pure food law, but guarantee the sale of same." The Bottling Works was located at 1210 Jefferson.

Photo Courtesy of Helen and Jean Klinefelter

In 1902, the year that Teddy Roosevelt went to the White House, a new courthouse was built on the east side. In 1900, civic agitation had begun for a new facility as citizens pointed with pride to the county's growth: 3,000 in 1857 when Waterloo got the first courthouse to 32,000 in 1900. With fighting spirit, Cedar Falls offered free land and a $50,000 grant to regain the courthouse they lost in 1855, but everyone was too focused on the east-west battle to pay much mind. The new courthouse, described as "French Renaissance" or "Grant Gothic" was built on property bounded by East Park Avenue, Lafayette, Sycamore and East Third. Six allegorical figures cast in bronze were set atop the courthouse to weather gracefully into "pea green goddesses" with everyone in the county wondering who or what the figures represented. In 1940, it was suggested the goddesses be used as scrap metal for the war effort but escaped destruction because they were "about the only art in the county."

Photo Courtesy of Waterloo Savings Bank

Plaid was popular at the turn of the century and until five or six years of age, little boys were dressed as little girls (boy on left). The older boy on the right is dressed in imitation of his father with the exception of his trouser length. Younger girls, too, wore dresses, shorter than their mothers'. Babies, in the 1880s, were dressed in long, flowing white dresses which changed to darker more practical dresses when they reached crawling age. Most clothes were homemade before 1900. Boys clothes were made from a durable, twilled serge brightened by white collars, white braid or fancy buttons. The toddler in the pram wore a cotton or soft lawn material. In the 1870s, it was considered "an abomination of the Lord" when little girls started wearing pantalets "just like men's attire". When the little girls' fashion gained acceptance, their mother's, too, ventured into the clothing realm of pantaloons.

Photo Courtesy of Mary Earle

In 1905, the east side business district looked like this. The mills still dominated the picture and there were lumber companies, wholesalers and other industries prospering along the river stretch. East Fourth was lined with stores but the Black Building and the First National Building had not yet been raised.

Photo Courtesy of Waterloo Public Library

Edward Kistner graduated from the Western College of Embalming and finished his professional training at the Chicago College of Funeral Directing in 1900. He was one of the first in Iowa to become licensed as a funeral director and embalmer. Two years later, he established Kistner Funeral Home at 517 Jefferson where Conway Inne now stands. Pictures were often taken then of the deceased in their coffins which gave rise to a spin-off business, "Kistner's highgrade picture framing and moulding". Prompt 24-hour ambulance service was also offered as you see written on the wagon. His second funeral home was opened in the 300 block of West Third Street near his home residence and undertaking parlor. The building still stands today. Mr. Kistner died in 1962.

Photo Courtesy of Don Durchenwald

Wood bending for sulkies was done on hand machines under the personal supervision of Samuel Jerald, founder of the Jerald Sulky Company. If a piece of inferior wood was used on the machine, it broke in two. Jerald was the only sulky builder who did his own wood bending to insure strength. Treatment of the wood, after the bending process, was done in a room where a temperature of 120 degrees and a relative humidity of 90 per cent was maintained. Samuel Jerald is shown third from the left, front row, with his work force at their location on Webster Street. William Card, with new facilities located on Wagner Road, now owns the company and reports that business is better than ever because of a renewed interest in horse and sulky racing.
Photo Courtesy of the Jerald Sulky Company

Nancy Hanks, one of the champion pacing horses in the 1890 era, used a new sulky to lower the mile record time from 2:09 to 2:05. The new invention was an attachment which allowed the high wheel sulky to use lower wheeled, pneumatic, ball bearing bicycle wheels to be placed on racing sulkies. Jerald first saw the sulky at the World's Fair in Chicago in 1893 and returned home to design a low wheeled sulky. He took out his patents and, before long, was busy making one sulky after another. At one time, there were at least a dozen sulky makers in the United States but by the crash of 1929 only two were left, Waterloo's Jerald Sulky and an Ohio firm. In the year following World War II, the Jerald Sulky Company enjoyed its most prosperous year, turning out just under 1000 sulkies with a retail value of $310 each. Photo shows workmen testing the strength of their product. It is now mandatory to use plastic discs over the spokes of the wheels to prevent horses from being injured. The sulkies presently retail at $900 and up.
Photo Courtesy of the Jerald Sulky Company

As the original settlers, the Mullans, Hannas and Virdens were all Methodist, Waterloo's first organized church organization was the First Methodist Society. Before a floor was even laid in the Mullan log cabin, Ashbury Collins, a Methodist circuit rider, conducted the first service in 1846 followed by other "horseback pastors." In 1855, the First Methodist Church of Waterloo transferred its regular meetings from pioneer homes to a seminary at Ninth and Bluff Streets and later alternated between Benight's Hall and Capwell's Hall on Commercial Street. By 1859, attendance had grown to 122. The first church, a two story building, was erected in 1862 on the corner of Jefferson and Fourth. In later years, augmented by 200 more members, the frame structure was bulging at the seams. A fine brick edifice was then raised on the corner of Fifth and Jefferson and was dedicated on February 16, 1890. The third building venture was the handsome facility at the corner of Fourth and Randolph. (photo) The night before dedication, on March 5, 1911, fire brought havoc to the new building; cleaning rags had ignited the blaze and caused $20,000 damage. After repair, the church dedication took place on July 9.
Photo from Waterloo: The Factory City

Is Jack Casebeer (right), flamboyant restauranteur and cigar manufacturer, hunting with friend, Jerry Hoyer, planning to serve the squirrels as hamburger meat in his eatery? Many oldtimers remember Casebeer's clever advertising such as when he took a photo of a crowd outside the I. C. depot and used it in an advertisement that read, "This is the crowd waiting to get inside Casebeer's Restaurant." Later linked to real estate, he developed Casebeer Heights now a part of Evansdale. To advertise his properties, he would paint signs on old car doors and nail them to trees in the neighborhood. Jack Casebeer was also one of the perpetrators of the infamous flying machine hoax. About 1900, a dirigible was placed by the river and Waterloo was led to believe it had just landed.
Photo Courtesy of Don Durchenwald

By 1904, 50 year-old Waterloo was boosting itself as the "Factory City". In population, the city had grown from 300 in 1854 to over 16,000 and was producing more than $20,000,000 in annual output of manufactured goods. The magic 15,000 population figure accorded Waterloo "first-class grade" in the rank of Iowa cities. Waterloo began its second fifty years by joining hands across the river to relish a rare unity and enjoy a "semicentennial" celebration. The west had the federal building and the east, the new courthouse and Carnegie was doling out for both an east and west library. Everybody, for a change was happy. The week long September hoop-la featured Gaskill's street carnival (one carnival camel escaped and was later found munching his way through a cabbage patch). The celebration committee apologized profusely because they were unable to resurrect a brace of oxen to pull the parade float depicting the 1845 covered wagon that brought the Hannas to town.
Photo Courtesy of Don Durchenwald

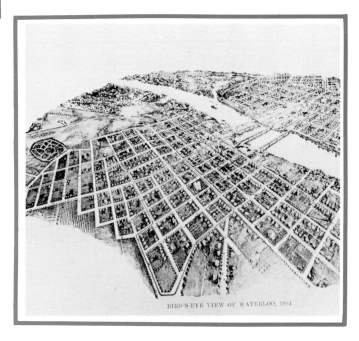

BIRD'S EYE VIEW OF WATERLOO, 1904

The first step taken in Waterloo for the establishment of public libraries was, on November 18, 1865, when the Waterloo Library Association formed in Dr. Mason's office. From 1867-1879, interest dwindled and the volumes accumulated were scattered. The society was revived in 1878 and the library, in 1892, was housed permanently in Brown's Opera House. In 1896, the library was then divided into two, one over the west side post office, the other on the second floor of the new city hall with almost 4,000 books listed in both locations. In the year 1905, Andrew Carnegie donated 30,000 dollars towards a Waterloo library. Because of east and west feuding, it was proposed the library be placed in the middle of the Cedar River. As the pot continued to boil, it was decided to lay the problem before the steel king himself who very graciously increased his bequest to $40,000, allowing a library to be built on each side, giving Waterloo distinction as the only city west of Pittsburgh with two libraries donated by Carnegie. Lots were acquired at West Fourth and South and Mulberry and East Fifth. The first head librarian, Fannie Duren, worked hard to promote the idea that the Waterloo Public Library was "one library housed in two buildings" and had her staff work part of each day at each library. Top photo shows the east library; bottom photo is the west library.

Library Photos Courtesy of Waterloo Public Library

Klinefelters rebuilt in brick, (adding a balcony), little forewarned of America's beginning love affair with the motor car. After World War I, there were no more livery stables in Waterloo but Klinefelters did stay on to stable area horses. Over the years, a handful of businesses would occupy the brick building on West Park Avenue and Jefferson but, on the west side of the building, you can still read the inscription "Klinefelters Livery", carved in stone.

Photo from the Klinefelter Collection

In 1906, a load of hay was delivered to Klinefelters Livery Stable (top photo). Two young boys playing in an alley discovered some hay spillage and set it on fire. Half an hour later, the blaze, fanned by a fierce northwest wind and fueled by combustibles in the stable, had destroyed Brown's Opera House, Klinefelters, two homes and two churches. Citizens fought "like Trojans" with two companies coming from Cedar Rapids. Damage was set at $50,000. Klinefelters lost a hearse, landaus and one ambulance. There was no loss of life only one horse (out of 70) by the name of "Prince".

Photo from the Klinefelter Collection

The need for a public hospital had long been felt in Waterloo and many efforts had been made to secure one. To ward off physician infighting, it was proposed to place the hospital under the charge of the Presbyterian Synod of Iowa. On May 1, 1903 a meeting was held at the Y.M.C.A. where fund canvasing and a search for a site got under way. The three story edifice housed an administration building, children's room, dining room, two rooms for non-paying patients and facilities to care for up to 40 patients. This stately looking hospital, located in the 1000 block of Leavitt Street, later became Woodlawn Nursing Home. It has now been razed and new condominiums stand on the site.

Photo Courtesy of Erma Lee and Gladys Stevens

The Waterloo Carriage Company built a buggy in this factory every twenty minutes which was pretty good for a staff of only 60 employees. The firm boasted that "all their departments were headed by men old enough to be full of experience but too young to be rutty". The company, established in 1902 and known as "The Great Line of the West", made cutters, delivery wagons, surreys and all kinds of buggies and runabouts. The products, sold by catalog and traveling salesmen, went all over the middle Western States and into Canada. Shipping the goods was not guaranteed past the crating. In advertising their superior product, Waterloo Carriage borrowed a "corny" line from Mark Twain. "As he said about his dog, 'It speaks for itself'."

Photo Courtesy of Leonard Katoski

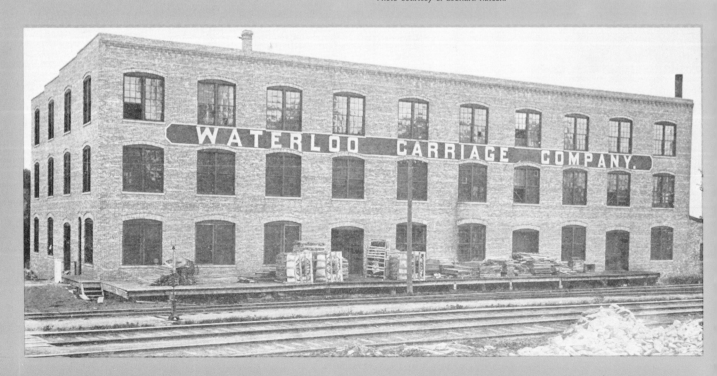

William Galloway, among other things, manufactured sulky plows and harrows. This sulky plow is being pulled by the "Iron Horse," which was guided by ropes and pulleys just like a team of horses would be driven. Galloway produced and promoted a harrow cart which he designed to carry a seated rider, freeing the farmer from the chore of walking behind a four-horse team. The first year the Galloway Company manufactured the harrows, 4,400 were sold and the following year, the grand total amounted to 7,700.

Photo Courtesy of Ross Galloway

William Galloway owned this large farm at what is now South Hackett Road and Highway 218. The "classy" barn, replacing an earlier one lost to fire, had the distinction of being the only one locally with a cement floored haymow. The silos were 50 by 20 feet and were made of hollow tile. Along with the harrow cart, the William Galloway Company also manufactured the manure spreaders (top photo), and cream separators giving Waterloo recognition as "The Home of the Great Wm. Galloway Company, the largest separator factory in the world." Much of the industrial development of Waterloo in the early 1900s centered around the dynamic "Will" Galloway.

Photo Courtesy of Ross Galloway

W. J. Peverill, a well-known Waterloo businessman, sold flour,
feed and fuel at 728 Lafayette Street and was listed as one of the
local coal distributors. He had a full supply of the best coal on the
market as well as fine feed and baled hay. His large flour business,
inventoried the best — bestselling brands. He employed eight
workers who gave prompt and careful attention to all customers.
His sales motto was "Call me (number CB) when you are cold or
your horse is hungry". This is a picture of William Peverill (with
mustache) during an afternoon drive in his Glide automobile.
Photo Courtesy of Micalea Lorenz

One of Galloway's loves which he fostered on his three Waterloo farms was livestock breeding. He scoured not only the countryside for registered cattle but also his native Scotland where he bought one hundred Ayrshires. His interest improved the quality of Northeast Iowa farming and he loaned out his purebred bulls to neighbors to upgrade their herds. Galloway once bought a $1,500 Holstein which he later sold for $40,000. The first Ayrshires the Universities of Nebraska, Louisiana and Kansas State ever owned came from the Galloway herds. Looking quite dashing at age 34, in 1912, William Galloway stands in front of his Mason-Maytag coupe showing his first Ayrshire bull calf. In 1910, Galloway persuaded Fred Maytag to put his Maytag car into production in Galloway's Waterloo plant, but because of a faulty rear axle, this venture failed.

Photo Courtesy of Ross Galloway

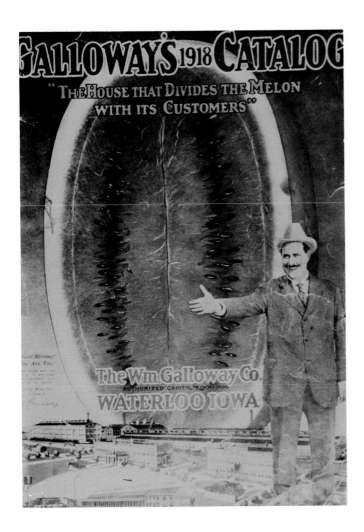

William Galloway after failing at interesting Montgomery Ward in putting his harrow cart in its catalog, decided to start his own mail order business which became one of the largest and best known in the country. Galloway knew how to sell both in person and in print. He selected his highly publicized watermelon logo while watching a wagon load of watermelons pass by his office window. The slogan, "The House that divides the melon with its customers" was to make the name Waterloo famous from coast to coast. The catalogs were sent all over the world, advertising household goods, clothing and cook stoves as well as farm implements.

Photo Courtesy of Don Durchenwald

William Galloway designed and manufactured the first Galloway tractor, the Farmobile. This 12-20, steel wheeled tractor retailed for $895 and was the top seller in his sales catalog. The tractor carried off the blue ribbon in the London Exposition competing against ten other American and European tractors. The Farmobile had the capacity to pull from three to five plows. Galloway manufactured over 1100 tractors during 1916 with $1.3 million worth shipped to Great Britain. When England defaulted on the bill to the tune of $450,000, Galloway, unable to meet his financial obligations, lost his business. He made a comeback in the seed business, specializing in Canadian oats, and in the manufacture of farm specialties, mainly oat hullers.

Photo Courtesy of Ross Galloway

Saturday was usually 'trip to town day'. The stores stayed open until late at night and the townspeople caught up on their socializing. But Sunday was everyone's day of rest. After church, in fine weather, a picnic such as this one along the beautiful Cedar River was the order of the day along with games like "Blind man's buff" and "Snap and catch'em". Obviously, romance was still in season year-round even back then.
Photo Courtesy of Don Durchenwald

Two beautiful Melan Arch bridges were built over the Cedar, one at Fourth Street in 1902-1903, (background) and a second in 1908 at Fifth Street. The Fourth Street tubular arch bridge had been removed to provide bridges crossing to Sans Souci and over Black Hawk Creek leaving only the Fifth Street bridge as a means of crossing the river in downtown Waterloo. The 1902 bridge, costing $74,000, was built of steel and cement, the steel being completely hidden in the cement giving the appearance of a solid stone block. This bridge, declared unsafe in 1974, was replaced at a cost of $990,000 the same year.
Photo from Waterloo: The Factory City

On its grand opening day, September 1, 1914, the owners of the $350,000 Russell-Lamson Hotel showed off the hotel's 250 rooms, 150 with bath, crowned with a richly appointed dining room and well-equipped kitchen. The hotel chef was, reputedly, one of the best in the state. On the mezzanine floor, hotel parlors and private dining rooms were located. The Russell-Lamson lobby, (photo) was magnificent for its day. The hotel has now been made into apartments with meeting rooms available.
Photo Courtesy of A. Bengston

This row of town houses stood facing East Fourth Street and the homes were regarded as quite elegant at the turn of the century. The Universalist Church of the Redeemer, site of the Strand Theater for many years, stands in the background. Some of these apartments still stand but have undergone a face lifting and, presently, offices are housed behind the new facade.
Photo Courtesy of Don Durchenwald

In 1912, autos like this Studebaker were up to their hubs in mud. William Galloway, the car owner, contributed $25,000 to help surface this muddy street with bituminous filled brick pavement, making it the first paved road between Waterloo and Cedar Falls.
Photo Courtesy of Ross Galloway

This photo of 1910 vintage shows a funeral procession on **Park** Avenue with Klinefelter's Livery Stable in the background. An auto and carriage company sits to the left of the stable and across the street was the Waterloo Laundry. Behind Klinefelters is the Lutheran Church at 427 ½ Jefferson, which was partially destroyed by fire in the Klinefelters, Brown's Opera blaze of 1906. The horse drawn hearses were rented from the livery stable. Klinefelters also rented automobile hearses (photo below) for funerals, black for adult and white for children. It seems that the widow in white preferred the horseless carriage as a more stately mode to bury her husband.

Photo Courtesy of Helen and Jean Klinefelter

F. C. Fish started the Fish Sign Service in a basement location at 519 Lafayette, adjacent Security Savings Bank. Almost every billboard in the Waterloo area sported the fish logo down in the corner of the sign. Frank Fish and his wife, Betty, were in the sign business for many years until they moved to California. Frank Fish, Jr. worked in partnership with his father. Frank and Betty Fish resided at 419 Lane Street while Frank, Jr. and wife, Ruth, lived at 927 Reber Avenue. The photo of the Fish family and friends was snapped in 1914.

Photo Courtesy of Kay Benston

CHAPTER III

1905-1940

When Erwin and Lenore Zeilinger were growing up at 201 Linwood Street, Waterloo was growing up, too. It was no longer the small railroad town their parents knew, but by 1900, Waterloo was well on its way to becoming a major manufacturing center. A souvenir booklet published in 1920 asserts:

"Here, on what has been declared to be the richest soil west of the Father of Waters, in the center of the great corn belt, the fame of which spreads 'round the world wherever hungry men and stock are fed, has been created by human hands one of the most remarkable manufacturing cities in the Middle West. What was hitherto a strictly agricultural community, and what is still surrounded by the most productive farmlands ever given to man out of the bounty of nature, has almost in the twinkling of an eye been transformed into a mighty workshop filled with throbbing machinery and clanging hammers."

The value of the city's manufactured goods had risen to 15 million compared with only two million in 1898. One hundred and fifty industries employed over 7,000 workers, producing 2,800 different items from a range of farm implements and machinery to fountain pens and women's skirts. And its population had jumped 112% in 10 years.

The fact that Waterloo had three railroads introduced many industries to the city and the industrial production, in return, brought big business to the railroads. Seventy-five trains entered Waterloo every twenty-four hours. Along with the electric railway, the railroads moved 75,000 cars of freight annually. People throughout the Midwest had heard and knew of Waterloo's bustling, thriving vitality.

It was the great age of boosterism. On the east side of the river was the Commercial Club and the Board of Trade. On the west, the Chamber of Commerce and the Waterloo Club. Each group worked for the improvement and embellishment of Waterloo, securing new industry and the dissemination of information. On each side of the river were the club rooms of each location, where the members could go for reading, recreation, card games or meals, or to entertain and regale visiting dignitaries.

Erwin and Lenore Zeilinger

Photo courtesy of Jean Lompe

There were, of course, the city builders. Men like Thomas Cascaden, Jr., Clyde Lamson, William Galloway and others. Lamson, Cascaden, and Galloway were the driving force behind the development of the Westfield Addition as a factory city. By 1904, there were some twenty industries located along the Waterloo, Cedar Falls and Northern tracks, including the J.S. Kemp Manufacturing Company, manufacturers of manure spreaders, the Waterloo Threshing Machine Company, Headford Brothers-Hitchens Foundry, Waterloo Self Feeders and Pump Company, the Waterloo Motor Works and Swift Manufacturing which made boilers, furnaces and iron castings. Galloway would also select this location to build his factory and agricultural club. Westfield was more than industry; the area between the factories and the river was also platted for home sites.

The bulk of Waterloo's industrial production was farm implements and machinery. Waterloo was the third largest producer of cream separators and manufactured one-fifth of all the stationary gasoline engines in the United States. Companies which produced these engines included Davis Engine, later merging with the Waterloo Gasoline Engine Company, the Iowa Gasoline Engine Company, Padden Manufacturing, Litchfield Manufacturing and the Associated Manufacturing Company. Associated built engines from one and one half to 12-horsepower, with popular names like the Chore Boy, Hired Hand, Twelve Mule Team. When farms had electricity, stationary gasoline engines became obsolete.

The service clubs of today had not yet appeared on the scene but there were organizations like the Town Criers and the Civic Society dedicated to boosting Waterloo. The Civic Society employed Charles Mulford Robinson, a contributing editor of Architectural Record, to look over the city and suggest ways to improve and enhance the city's image. He recommended that the poles supporting the trolley lines be painted a dark color to make them less conspicuous; utility lines be buried; shabby waste cans and unattractive horse watering troughs discarded and attractive greenery and shubbery placed in school yards and in front of public buildings. He suggested the city implement a building code and appoint a river front commission to improve the riverbank's appearance. He pinpointed two problems that would plague Waterloo for years to come — railroad tracks crisscrossing the city and the need for a new city hall. Waterloo went to work on many of his suggestions but a new city hall had to wait for fifty years. Mr. Robinson realized that Waterloo was a city, not joined but divided by a river. In his report he wrote:

"There seems to be only one danger that seriously threatens the advance of Waterloo in municipal aesthetics and effectiveness. That is the lack of complete union between the east side and the west, of the whole souled cooperation which forgets itself in the greatness of a common task."

At this time, Waterloo had two separate school systems on either side of the river and a public library for each side. A public building placed on the east side had to be balanced with one on the west. The courthouse on the east side meant that the post office had to go on the west. To choose a site for a new city hall without a counter balancing structure for compromise was impossible. Building in the middle of the river was given serious consideration.

With growth of industry, Waterloo lost its small town image. Taller buildings appeared on the west side — the Russell-Lamson Hotel, the Pioneer Bank Building and the Black Hawk Bank Building. In 1914, the Russell-Lamson Building which housed the Paul Davis Department Store burned down and was not rebuilt until 1926. Across the river, Black's Department Store built an impressive ten story building. The First National Bank and the Commercial Bank were located in sizable structures and the Lafayette Building was just a block up the street. The Waterloo, Cedar Falls & Northern trolley lines made all parts of the city to the downtown area easily accessible.

The great flood of immigrants from Europe to America reached clear back to the small cities of the Midwest. Germans and Austrians had been coming to Waterloo since the mid 1870's and were, by far, the largest foreign group. Der Deutsch Amerikaner, a German language weekly newspaper was published in Waterloo from 1872 to 1917 and in 1910, claimed there were over 25,000 German speaking people in Black Hawk county.

Jews, escaping the pogroms of Russia, were not a large group but a number came to set up shop as small businessmen. The Sons of Jacob Synagogue was organized about 1906 with a small temple building at 611 West Fifth. Today, their temple at 411 Mitchell, is a handsome structure. The Greeks coming to Waterloo via Chicago were looking and hoping to find improved working conditions. They worked at the packing plant and on the railroads. In 1914, they organized the Hellenic Orthodox Church of St. Demetrios and, four short years later, acquired the property on West Fourth Street where the present church is located. At one time the Greek community, numbering in the neighborhood of 2,000 persons, represented the largest Greek colony in Iowa. Today, only 150 people of Greek origin reside locally.

Blacks began coming to Waterloo around 1911. Some came to replace striking workers in the Illinois Machine shops while others hoped to find better jobs in the factories of the north. Blacks presently comprise ten percent of the population.

The wonderful world of entertainment took on new face and character when the movie houses took over. Saturday matinees, the children were drawn to Hoot Gibson and Tom Mix westerns with the parents spending the evening enjoying Gloria Swanson, Pola Negri and Rudolph Valentino. Everybody adored Mary Pickford. Radio came in during the twenties and gave the movie industry some cause for concern.

Like the rest of the country, Waterloo fell prey to the automobile. It provided a mobility that trains and streetcars could not match. Iowans took to the roads, paved or unpaved. The Sunday afternoon drive became a cherished institution.

By 1928, Waterloo's population had reached 40,000. Two thousand were employed by the railroads and 6,000 by 160 industrial plants. There were 21 jobbing houses, 50,000 carloads of freight were moved annually, down a third from 1915. The city had 76 miles of paved streets, 90 miles of sewer, 75 miles of water mains and the county recorded 16,000 autos in operation.

The good times came to a crashing halt when the bubble burst on Wall Street in 1929. As the economic depression deepened, Waterloo had the distinction of being the hardest hit city of its size in the nation. John Deere closed down but Rath's was able to keep workers on the job. The Salvation Army and the Red Cross were over taxed and over burdened by those in need. In a period of five months, the Salvation Army reported serving 10,500 meals with a food wagon sent to outlying areas such as Riverview Addition. Six hundred families received clothing. The Red Cross distributed 35 hundred barrels of flour and 20,000 yards of cloth. Volunteers also sewed clothing for the needy and, with large nets, seined fish from the river for food. Corn plunged from 90¢ a bushel to 12¢. Hogs brought $2.35 a hundred weight and cattle $4.50. Eggs cost 8 cents a dozen, and hamburger, 10 cents a pound. Children hung around the railroads and heckled the train crews into throwing coal at them. Others scavenged around dumps for old tires to burn for warmth.

In an effort to restore banking and economic stability, on March 6, 1933, President Roosevelt closed all banks in the nation from Monday to Thursday. Only one bank in Waterloo survived the four day holiday — the Waterloo Savings Bank located on the corner of Fourth and Commercial. The Pioneer, the Black Hawk, The First National and the Commercial closed their doors permanently. With the assets of the Commercial bank and the help of the Reconstruction Finance Corporation, a group of businessmen organized a new bank — the National Bank of Waterloo. It opened for business in June at the site of the First National Bank at Sycamore and Fourth with assets of over one million. The first day, Rath's deposited $50,000. The Black Hawk County Treasurer deposited $40,000. Waterloo had now been reduced from 12 banking facilities in 1910, to two.

Recovery was slow and painful. The depression dragged on through the thirties. It would take the wartime economy of the forties to rev up industry and provide full employment.

This view of Fourth Street was taken from the Irving Hotel corner looking across the bridge to the east side business district. The block between Commerical and the bridge was called Bridge Street. Across from the hotel, the Waterloo Savings Bank (right foreground with canopied windows) had its first home. The Henderson Drug company was also located here as were other drug stores. In the seventies, all the buildings you see on this side of the street were torn down to allow for a relocation of Fourth Street and the bridge. The large building on the right before the bridge is the Syndicate Block. Across the bridge, the word FIRST is visible and denotes the site of the First National Bank. Across the street you can catch a glimpse of the Union Flour Mill.

Photo (Circa 1916) Courtesy of Matt Parrott and Sons Printing Company

When the packing plant that E. F. Rath and his father owned in Dubuque burned down, some Waterloo businessmen suggested he rebuild in their town. After all, they argued, Waterloo was more in the center of the hog raising portion of the state. Rath's accepted their logic and, in 1891, built their packing plant on Elm Street, near the river where they could cut ice for refrigeration. Initially, Rath's employed 22 workers and bought $100,000 worth of livestock their first year in business here. The Rath Packing Company is probably the oldest firm in Waterloo still doing business at its original location.

Photo Courtesy of Waterloo Public Library

The hard-working crew first procured by Rath's are pictured with their handiwork in the background. In those days, to make ham the men soaked the meat in hogsheads of brine for 40 to 80 days before smoking it. Today, curing fluid is injected and then the meat is smoked within a few days. John Rath is the young man in the middle wearing a suit. A cousin of E. F. Rath and recent graduate from a Chicago business school, John joined the firm as bookkeeper and manager and worked his way up to president (1898-1943). Members of the Rath family served as company presidents until 1964. Reuben, the son of E. F. Rath, succeeded John from 1943 to 1950, followed by John's son, Howard, the last Rath president to reign.

Photo Courtesy of Waterloo Public Library

The Powers Manufacturing Company is a good example of a business that has been able to survive because it changed with the times. In 1902, L. J. Powers was running a general store in Powersville near Nashua, Iowa. He sold horse collars made in the south which were filled with cotton lint. The cottonseed oil contained in the lint seemed to have a healing effect on the sores that developed on horses' necks. Mr. Powers, requesting the right to manufacture these collars in Iowa, opened a factory at 1340 Sycamore and has been at that locale ever since. Since their horse collar manufacturing days the company has made pretty much anything that can be worked on a sewing machine. During World War I, it was canteen and wagon covers and tents for the armed services. In World War II, they made officers' shirts and fatigue jackets. In ensuing years, they stitched up shirts and work clothes. At the present time, they specialize mainly in athletic clothing.

Photo Courtesy of Powers Manufacturing Company

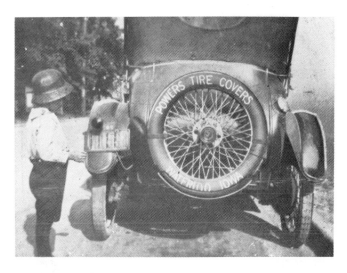

In the 1920's, Mr. Powers of Powers Manufacturing which made horse collars, decided to branch out in other lines, such as making work clothes for Sears and Montgomery Ward. Powers also started a line of automobile accessories, and manufactured such items as top recovers, radiator protectors and tire covers. If you wanted, you could order tire covers with advertising written across. Powers sold the successful auto accessories line to the Hinson Manufacturing Company and it was their major production for many years.

Photo Courtesy of Powers Manufacturing Company

Their athletic equipment includes everything from warm-up clothes to basketball shorts. The purchase of knitting machines from an Illinois mill allowed them to expand their line to include knit garments. Powers has the distinction of being the first to design and manufacture the striped black and white referee's shirt now worn almost universally by referees for most team sports.

Photo Courtesy of Powers Manufacturing Company

"Teddy" Roosevelt visited Waterloo twice, once as vice-president during the 1900 campaign and again as president. The first time around, he spoke in Lincoln Park before a crowd estimated at 40,000. Special excursion trains brought people from as far as Des Moines to see and hear the popular outspoken vice-president. Probably very few heard his words as his voice had become strained from the long speaking tour. The second visit, shown in this photo occurred June 2, 1903, after Roosevelt had become president, after the assassination of President McKinley. It was hoped that the president would again be able to address the crowds in the park but his tight "whistle stop" schedule only permitted a 10 minute speech from the train's platform at the old Illinois Central Depot. A speaker's stand was erected for the president at the station but the crowds were too great for him to reach it.

Photo from Waterloo Savings Bank Publication

Cars outnumber the horse drawn vehicles in this view of West Fourth Street. The Leavitt and Johnson Bank (the large building in the center) later changed its name to the Pioneer Bank. Along the street to the right you see a horse drawn van from Altstadt and Langlas Bakery delivering Kleenmaid Bread to a store or cafe. At this period in time, the poles supporting the trolley wires were painted white. When Charles Mulford Robinson, a contributing editor of the Architectural Record, was invited by the Civic Society to come to Waterloo and suggest ways to improve the city's facial features, one of his suggestions was to paint the poles a dark color so they would be less obtrusive.

Photo Courtesy of Matt Parrott and Sons Printing Company

When Charles Robinson made his report in 1910 to the Civic Society of Waterloo, he recommended that the city appoint a river front commission to improve the riverbank's appearance. This photo of the east side of the river between Fourth and Fifth Street Bridges inclines the viewer to agree. The large, dark structure on the left proclaiming "Use Clear Quill Flour" was the warehouse of the Union Mill which was torn down in the twenties and supplanted by the Paramount Theater in 1926. Palace Clothiers was advertising an east side location. Some yeas later, they would move to the west side. During this era, Waterloo had two telephone exchanges; the Corn Belt Exchange (building at the far right) was one of them and serviced 8,000 phones in Waterloo and 25 surrounding communities, even providing long distance service within a 50-mile radius. In more recent times, the Exchange Building has been used as an apartment house set off by several small businesses on the ground floor.

Photo Courtesy of Matt Parrott and Sons Printing Company

In 1892, John Froelich (left) of Froelich, Iowa ran a grain elevator and made extra money on the side threshing in Iowa and South Dakota. His steam engine was noisy, clumsy, hard to move and apt to set fire to the grain. Froelich envisioned building a gasoline powered traction engine or tractor that would eliminate such dangers and inconvenience. With a helper, William Mann, he put together a sort of hybrid machine which stubbornly refused to work on its trial run. Mann wedged a rifle cartridge (without the bullet) into the priming cup, hit it with a hammer, and the flywheel set to spinning. Froelich put the machine in gear and it moved forward. He put it in reverse and, clankety clank, it moved backwards. He and Mann had invented the first gasoline tractor (below). Froelich took it to South Dakota that year and made a small fortune threshing 72,000 bushels of grain!

Photo Courtesy of Deere and Company

QUEST

2018 29 Street
Rock Island
Illinois 61201

In introducing this publication, we learned that many Waterloo residents were strongly impressed by the original artwork used on our dust jacket cover. The cover was reproduced from a pastel painting by noted Waterloo artist, Gary Kelley. Gary has capably captured the essence of life, a truly memorable representation of early Waterloo: the romance of the Cedar in combination with the omnipresent smokestacks of Waterloo industry.

We are pleased to offer a limited edition lithograph of this handsome piece of art entitled <u>Along the Cedar</u>. The printing is limited to 250 numbered reproductions. They are available on a first come, first served basis. Particular numbers will be reserved, if possible, otherwise number appointment will be at random. Your lithograph will be hand delivered to ensure proper care and protection. The cost is $25 per print unframed.

This lithograph is printed on museum quality pH neutral paper. The size is nineteen inches by twenty-six inches.

Please send me # _____ of 250 Gary Kelley paintings entitled <u>Along the Cedar</u>. Another number will be suitable if above is taken. I have enclosed check or money order for

	$25.00
4% sales tax	$ 1.00
Total	$26.00

Deliver to

_____
Name

_____
Address

_____

_____ (Phone)

Mail to Quest Publishing, 2018 29 Street, Rock Island IL 61201

QUEST PUBLISHING

2018-29TH STREET-ROCK ISLAND, ILLINOIS 61201-(309) 794-0505

This wide-eyed, little farm boy is pointing out the merits of the stationary gasoline engine down on the farm; how it can be used to pump water for animals, (as in the picture) for grinding feed or even used as a power source. Today, most farms are supplied with electricity and the stationary gasoline engine is a collector's item. In 1896, the company brought out an improved tractor but the world wasn't ready for it and only one sold. Next, the company tried to manufacture two-cylinder automobiles but increased demand for stationary engines effectively terminated the project after only six cars had been sold.

Photo Courtesy of Deere and Company

Twenty men, in 1895, made up the work crew of the Waterloo Gasoline Engine Company, located on the corner of Third and Cedar Streets. The crew continued to try and develop a salable tractor but the mainstay of their business was the stationary engine. In this arena, the men in overalls exhibited such expertise and the demand was so great that, by 1910, they needed a bigger factory. At the new facility, located on the corner of Miles and Commercial Streets, the work force eventually grew to include 1,000 men.

Photo Courtesy of Robert Levis

Deere continued to manufacture the Waterloo Boy Model until 1923 at which time they came out with their own model D, one of the most popular and dependable tractors ever built. It could cover 15 acres a day with a disc tiller, 100 acres with a single disc and operate a 28-inch thresher. The familiar putt-putt sound of its two-cylinder engine would be heard around the nation and around the world for many years to come.

Photo Courtesy of Deere and Company

The "try, try again" spirit paid off when, in 1913, the Waterloo Gasoline Engine Company introduced a successful tractor with a two-cylinder engine. That year, twenty machines were sold and not one returned. The following year, they brought out an improved model — the first Waterloo Boy single speed tractor. An incredible 118 machines sold in 1914, and by 1918, the figure was well over 8,000. Deere and Company of Moline kept a close eye on the progress of the Waterloo Engine Company and its growing success. At tractor trials all around the country, the Waterloo Boy out plowed and out maneuvered its competition. Anxious to add a quality tractor to their line, Deere bought the Waterloo Engine Company in 1918, to the tune of $2,100,000.

Photo Courtesy of Deere and Company

Step number two for John Froelich was to organize a factory to manufacture the gasoline tractors. Froelich chose Waterloo because of its rail service and strong work force. He called his wood frame factory the Waterloo Gasoline Traction Engine Company. The first two tractors sold were returned. Thus, the company decided to manufacture stationary gasoline engines while contributing to experiment with tractors. Froelich wasn't interested in building stationary engines so he withdrew from the company. It was reorganized by George Miller under the name of the Waterloo Gasoline Engine Company in 1895.

Photo Courtesy of Deere and Company

One summer's day in 1931 at the John Deere plant on Westfield, they lined up these eleven farm tractors and took their picture. Compared to today's behemoths, these machines resemble garden tractors. This was 13 years after John Deere had taken over the old Waterloo Gasoline engine factory and 8 years since they had brought out the Model D. John Deere was, at this time, considerably larger than the original plant and would continue to grow until it spread all along that portion of Westfield. The tiny park where this photo was taken has disappeared with the expansion.

Photo Courtesy of Deere and Company

When Chautauqua was in full swing during the hot weather, the campers in Cedar River Park could always go to the beach nearby to cool off. At that time, there were no public swimming pools, but the park maintained a bathhouse for changing clothes and the Shoot which was obviously the quickest way for a timid bather to splash into the water. No one gave a care, in those days, as to whether the water was polluted or not.

The first public pools were built at Byrnes and Gates Parks shortly after the end of World War II. By then, the bathhouse at Cedar River Park had been torn down and swimming in the river was no longer in style.

Photo Courtesy of Waterloo Public Library

Around the turn of the century, the high point of summer living in and around Waterloo was the Chautauqua. For a full week, the townspeople could come out and enjoy a program of music, speakers, variety entertainment, and old-time religion. The Chautauqua Association was organized in 1892 as part of the promotion of a group of businessmen to develop the Sans Souci area as a summer resort. Known as the Cedar River Park Association, the group had bought 40 acres on which to build summer homes. The first Chautauqua program lasted for ten days and was housed in a tent. Even though the talent was mostly local, it was so successful that the following year a 2000 seat amphitheater was built. When this was damaged by flood, a larger building called the Coliseum replaced it. Chautauquas originated in Chautauqua, New York, where a summer school for Sunday School teachers had been established in 1874. The school always included programs of secular interest and were so popular, towns all over the nation copied the idea. Travelling Chautauquas grew up to provide speakers and entertainment to the local associations. William Jennings Bryan won great popularity on this circuit and also appeared in Waterloo.

Photo Courtesy of the Waterloo Public Library

J. J. Meany began making caskets in a barn in his backyard in 1922. When he moved to this building on Falls Avenue, he shared it with several other businesses. Gradually he took over the entire building and then added to it. This aerial view of the plant shows the neighborhood the way it was before the relocation of highway 218. Beyond the Meany plant can be seen the John Deere factory on Westfield. Three generations of the Meany family have operated the factory.

Photo Courtesy of Meany Casket Company

In their packing crates, the finished caskets are about to be trucked to the railroad freight house. The large building which can be seen beyond the factory is old fire station #4 which stood on the corner of Falls Avenue and Oak Lawn and was torn down to make way for highway 218. The highway at one time went out of town on Falls. It was relocated to the west when it became a four-lane.

Photo Courtesy of Meany Casket Company

Originally all the caskets were made of hardwood — oak, walnut or mahogany. Their first caskets were made of cypress and then covered with fabric. The fancy liners were tufted and sewn in the sewing room. In this picture, workers are fitting lids on wooden caskets. Since 1950, all caskets have been made of metal, bronze, copper and iron according to the specifications of the funeral director. There is a lot of hand work in finishing a casket — about 50 man hours. Production amounts to five or six caskets a day.

Photo Courtesy of Meany Casket Company

In this Flint photograph, you are looking west across Fourth Street Bridge toward Commercial Street. The Syndicate Block is on the left with the Majestic Theater in the rear. Theater patrons entered from the front of the Syndicate Building. A turkish bath is located on the building's corner. Across the street is the YMCA which was replaced in 1932. A little bit of the stone foundation of the mill built orginally on the Y site can be seen at the right. Down the street you see Davidsons, a furniture store which would later take over the Syndicate Building.

Photo Courtesy of Matt Parrott and Sons Printing Company

When Flint took this picture about 1917, the Russell-Lamson Hotel had been christened a few short years before. The spire belonged to a church built by the Congregationalists who sold their place of worship to the Baptists before raising their present church on South and Fourth Streets. The large building on the right is Black Hawk County Memorial Hall which opened in December of 1916. Iowa law allows local government to build such structures to commemorate and serve the armed services as well as furnishing a meeting place for all patriotic organizations. Today, seventeen different groups use the facility. In 1964, Waterloo planned to tear down the hall, use the space for parking and build a new memorial building near the present Recreation Center. Funds were not forthcoming so Memorial Hall lives on, continuing to serve our nation's veterans.

Photo Courtesy of Matt Parrott and Sons Printing Company

When the Litchfield Manufacturing Company opened its Waterloo plant in 1904, they promised "the complete manufacturing plant, considering beauty and solidity of buildings and consideration of the comfort, health and pleasure of its employees." The five buildings on ten acres had side walls made of solid stone, with the building front in dressed limestone, pressed brick and artificial stone trimming. It boasted a fire proof roof — three thicknesses of 24 pound wool felt soaked in asphalt and laid in asphalt and 600 windows provided plenty of light with ribbed glass to cut down on glare. For the workers' comfort, the air in the foundry was changed every 90 seconds. Near the foundry, showers were available so that workers could clean up before wending homeward. The importance and prominence of the plant to the Waterloo citizenry is indicated by the fact that the trolley which brought workers to and from the factory was called the "Litchfield".

Photo found in early publication

The Litchfield Company made a variety of farm implements such as grinders, forges, anvils, and manure spreaders as shown in the top photo. For a time, they also produced washing machines (bottom photo). It was a successful firm until the twenties when bad management caused it to go out of business. The Schultz Company, manufacturing a line of farm machinery, took over the factory and continued in business for a number of years.

Photo Courtesy of Don Durchenwald

These serious thirteen year-olds are members of the First Lutheran confirmation class of 1909. Their church home had been built only two years earlier. The Lutheran congregation was organized in 1867 and originally met in other churches or in meeting halls. In 1872, they built their first church on Jefferson Street in back of Browns Opera House, next to Klinefelters livery stable, but the fire which destroyed the Opera House, damaged the stable and church. Since most of their membership lived on the east side of town, they chose to relocate and build a larger church at Maple and High streets. Their present church is the second building on this site. Celebrating their centennial, the members held special services at the original location, now converted to a parking lot.

Photo Courtesy of Jean Lompe

THE "MAYTAG," MODEL C (Formerly the "Mason") FIVE PASSENGER CAR.

THE SWIFT, SIMPLE, DEPENDABLE CAR FOR COUNTRY AND CITY.

PRICE, WITHOUT TOP...... $1,350.00

Exhorted by William Galloway, Fred Maytag, a former Iowa senator brought his car, the Maytag-Mason, to Waterloo from Newton and set up his manufacturing firm in a building owned by Galloway. A man named Mason had developed the Mason car with the help of Fred Duesenberg who would later become famous for the car named in his honor. Galloway and Mason bought out the Mason Car Company and called their new product the Maytag-Mason. Later they changed the name simply to Maytag.
Photo Courtesy of Don Durchenwald

Advertising for the Maytag auto always emphasized its ability to climb grades. Here it is shown climbing the steps of the Iowa State Capitol in Des Moines. Its ability to climb hills could not disguise the fact that the car was faulty in design and many were returned to the factory. But one satisfied 1907 buyer, according to the Maytag advertisement, drove his Maytag model 4,000 miles and only required 40 cents in auto repairs over that distance. Maytag closed the Waterloo plant and went to Newton to make farm implements and later washing machines. Eventually, the ex-senator, known for his upright business dealings, paid off all the shareholders who lost money on the Maytag auto venture.
Photo Courtesy of Ron Lampe

While it was located in Waterloo, the Dart Truck Company built four different trucks ranging from ½-ton to 3½-ton capacity. The photo shows a sampling of their line including fire engines, a variety of delivery vans and omnibuses. During World War I, Dart supplied the army with 2-ton trucks. In 1920, the firm added farm tractors to their production line.

Dart Truck along with Ford was founded in 1903 in Anderson, Indiana. Initially, Dart manufactured solid-tire, high-wheel, ½-ton wagon-type trucks powered by a 2-cylinder, 25-horsepower gasoline engine which allowed the vehicle to do up to 27 mph on a good road. In 1907, the company was moved to Waterloo where it expanded its line and built a reputation as a pioneer of quality trucks. During the twenties, company ownership changed hands and the plant was moved to Kansas City, Missouri where it is still located. Today the Dart Truck Company specializes in off the highway, heavy-duty equipment. They build front end loaders, bottom dump trucks, and aircraft refuelers.

Photo Courtesy of Dart Truck Company

Waterloo's biggest annual event is the National Cattle Congress Fair held in September. It combines all the features of a county fair — prize livestock, farm machinery, carnival rides, commercial and agricultural exhibits, flower and garden shows, horse and tractor pulls, nationally known entertainers — all on a gargantuan scale with crowds to match. Its 1982 attendance was 220,295. Only the Iowa State Fair rivals this attraction.

It began inauspiciously as a dairy cattle show with 40,000 attending. Few dairy farmers bothered to attend the annual meeting of the Iowa Dairy Association. So the officers suggested that a concurrent dairy show might be a draw. The experiment was successfully tested at the 1909 Cedar Rapids meeting. The next year, Waterloo was to play host and Hugh Van Pelt, show director, determined that the Waterloo show would be so successful, the city would win the honor of becoming the permanent site. Van Pelt personally made sure that 13 carloads of

prize cattle came directly from the Illinois State Fair to highlight the Waterloo show.

Chautauqua Park was the site selected. The coliseum housed the prize dairy cattle — Holsteins, Jerseys, Guernseys and Ayrshire — as well as displays of dairy machinery. Four large tents displayed other kinds of farm implements. There was a special tent for judging animals and a tent for the Dairy Association to hold their meetings. A merry-go-round, some side shows and a few food stands rounded out the show.

The quality of the stock on display was excellent with several animals valued as high as $15,000. Exhibitors were thrilled to sell their stock at good prices. Farm machinery, too, sold well, with salesmen making more sales in a week than they had in an entire year!

Photo Courtesy of National Cattle Congress Fair

The Waterloo members convinced the State Dairy Cattle Association that their city was the best location for the next year's (1912) show. Local businessmen pitched in and offered to assume all work responsibilities and to provide prize money. In 1912, a permanent show site of 10 acres was acquired and a corporation called The Dairy Cattle Congress was formed. The Congress constructed two buildings with a canvas stretched between to

serve as an extra pavilion. Each year, the show grew impressively with new departments and new buildings added. In 1917, and 1919, respectively, a Saddle Horse and Belgian Horse Show were included. The 1949 program committee pinned on blue ribbons in a host of divisions such as — poultry, waterfowl, home canned goods, rabbits, textiles and antiques plus corn, alfalfa and soybean exhibits.

Photo Courtesy of National Cattle Congress Fair

Cluster lights illuminated most of the downtown area in 1916. Mr. Robinson, in his capacity as city beautification critic, disappoved of the many advertising signs overhanging the sidewalk. The buildings along the right side of the street today are minus the decorative cornices and window trims. Walker's Shoe Store is in the first floor of the three story building. The Golden Rule, owned by J. E. and A. L. Ferguson, carried wallpaper, china, glassware and kitchen furnishings. The Columbia theater was a miniature movie house the same size as a store with rows of benches set out for patrons. Across the street, you can see the YWCA, located upstairs over a cafeteria. The YWCA building on Lafayette was not built until 1922.

Photo Courtesy of Matt Parrott and Sons Printing Company

When the new courthouse was built on the corner of Park Avenue and Sycamore in 1906, the county also provided a home for the sheriff right next door. He could never be very far away from the criminals in his charge — as the jail was attached to the back of his house. The present courthouse on Fifth Street has the jail on the top floor and the sheriff is no longer personally on twenty-four hour duty.

Photo from Black Hawk County Atlas, 1910

By 1910, the police department had grown to 15 men plus the chief. Gone were the "Keystone Cop" helmets. Except for the badges they wore, the police corps looked more like a group of railway conductors than lawmen. No one knows what the status of the dog was.

Photo from Black Hawk County Atlas, 1910

In a time when decor was not too vital to a restaurant, the Krimnitz Bakery was a pleasant place for a bite to eat. The tempting smell of fresh baked Danish and German coffee cakes emanating around the neighborhood and their promise to serve up lunch and meals at any time of the day surely attracted a hearty clientele. The stamped metal ceiling is interesting but not unusual as most retail businesses had similar ceilings in this era.

Photo from Black Hawk County Atlas, 1910

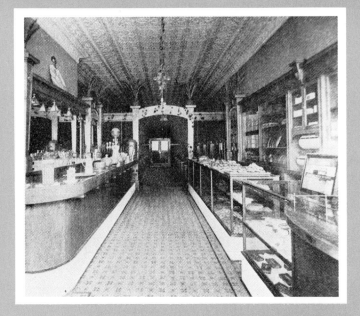

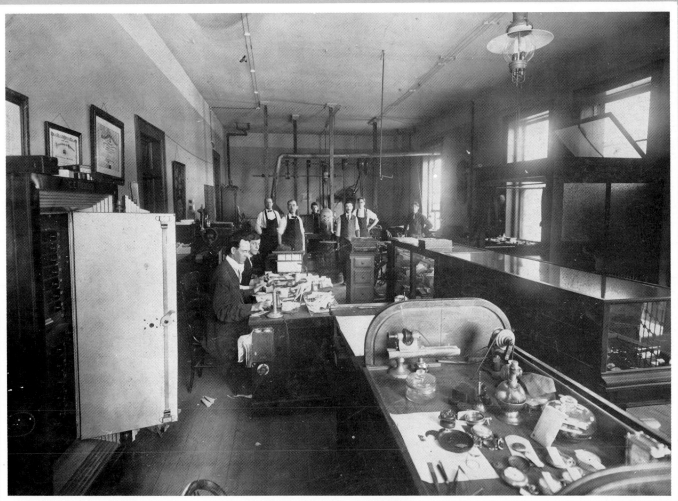

Around 1900, Julius Levi operated a jewelry manufacturing business on the second floor of a store located at Lafayette and Fourth Street. He not only made jewelry but also trained workers to repair watches. Julius is the man standing behind the file cabinet. Some of the workers in the photo have been identified as C. E. Frederick, Carl Imhoff, Frank Knapp, and Arthur Knapp. Julius' two sons also became jewelers and their shop, Levi Brothers Jewelry and Loan Company, is still owned by Mr. and Mrs. Jay Levi at 304 Fourth Street.

Photo Courtesy of Mrs. Jay Levi

The American Red Cross came to Iowa in 1916 under the guidance of a Cedar Falls physician, Dr. Lillie A. Arnett. The next year the organization put on a tremendous push for new members using all kinds of entertainment stunts, auctions and parades to encourage citizens to join. With the slogan on ambulances "Let the spirit of '76 be the spirit of '17" inciting stars and stripes patriotism, this group of local businessmen in "Paul Revere" cocked hats went out to beat the bushes to drive in new members.

Statewide, the drive was successful with 140 chapters organized and 67% of Iowa's population belonging to the Red Cross. The war brought out the "red, white and blue" spirit in everyone and what could be more patriotic than to belong to the organization that did so much for our men in the armed forces.

In 1918, the great influenza epidemic struck and the local Red Cross chapter helped the nuns of St. Francis Hospital equip Memorial Hall as a temporary hospital. They also organized a motor corps to take victims to the hospital.

Early programs included first aid and home nursing courses. In 1920, the chapter acquired two rooms in the YMCA for headquarters. That year, the association also organized the disaster relief commission.

Today, the current Red Cross program includes services to the armed forces and veterans, disaster relief, blood collection, teaching first aid, swimming and lifesaving classes, small craft safety, nursing services and a youth program.

Photo Courtesy of Robert Levis

By 1910, Waterloo had two fire stations: one on the east side (top left) on Fifth Street next to the library and one on the west (top right), on Commercial between Fifth and Sixth. Three horse drawn fire engines were kept at the east station, as well as an extension ladder long enough to reach the top story of most buildings in Waterloo. The east fire chief had his own automobile. The picture shows ten firemen along with the fire chief. The west side station had two fire engines and a crew of nine. Fire alarm boxes were located throughout the city allowing citizens to alert the department to fire danger.
Photo from Black Hawk County Atlas, 1910

The Soash Land Company, with W. P. Soash as "The Empire Builder," maintained lavish offices in Waterloo for the purpose of encouraging Iowans to give up their own green pastures for greener ones in the "fertile" Big Springs Country on the southern plains of Texas. They were in the business of "colonization and immigration" to the "lands of opportunities." Although Waterloo was their home office, they also manned plush offices in Plainview, Texas, Des Moines, Madison, Wisconsin, and Minneapolis, Minnesota. They had an operating force of 500 salesmen. Twice a month, "The Empire Builder" organized excursion trains for would-be land buyers. Rail cars were located in different places in the north central states and linked up into a train at Kansas City.
Photo from Black Hawk County Atlas, 1910

In the days when home laundry meant scrubbing on a washboard and boiling white clothes in a copper kettle, the commercial laundry was one way to escape the tedium. The Model Laundry at Fourth and Mulberry did a big enough business to require three delivery rigs. The Model was in business for some years after World War II before automatic washing machines and laundromats cut into the commercial laundry business.
Photo Courtesy of Don Durchenwald

James E. Sedgwick, lawyer, real estate developer, founder of an abstract company and president of the Leavitt and Johnson Bank bought Sedgwick Island in 1884 to build a summer home. He purchased a sand dredger and built up his island by dumping sand and dirt on it from the river. In 1912, he built a permanent residence there which featured a 15-foot fireplace that devoured 4-foot logs. A special elevator was installed to bring the logs from the basement to the living room.

Sedgwick died in 1918 but his daughter, Mrs. Andrew Reid, continued to live on the island until her death in 1943. Subsequently, the house was turned into a nightclub called "The Island." John Deere Company bought the property in 1954. The island has now disappeared, incorporated into the expansion of the John Deere Component Works. A four lane street now carries traffic to and from the John Deere plant over the spot where the Sedgwick home once stood.

Photo Courtesy of Don Durchenwald

The photo shows a Powers Manufacturing Company workroom in the days when the firms chief product was horse collars. The young ladies are operating machines that riveted metal parts such as buckles to fabric. They were paid 16¢ an hour and probably worked a 60 hour week.

Photo Courtesy of Helen and Jean Klinefelter

When the family first lived on the island, there was no bridge access. The Sedgwicks forded the river with a horse and buggy. When the dam raised the level of the river permanently, two bridges were built, one at Whitney Road and another at Duryea Street.

Photo Courtesy of Don Durchenwald

Most young men marching off to war took time to have their pictures taken in uniform. Art Theimer going overseas in World War I was no exception. The studio even supplied a suitable backdrop — a military encampment. This photograph went to Art's girl, to remember him by.

Photo Courtesy of Jean Lompe

When members of the Rainbow Division came home from France in 1919, the soldiers detrained in a Waterloo decorated top to bottom with flags, rainbows and ribbons. From the Great Western Station, they paraded triumphantly through the city. Dinner and entertainment were bountifully provided before the troops returned to their train for the trip to Des Moines and demobilization. The Rainbow Division, whose casualties totalled more than 14,000, served with distinction in France, fighting at Chateau-Thierry and Sedan.

Photo Courtesy of Waterloo Public Library

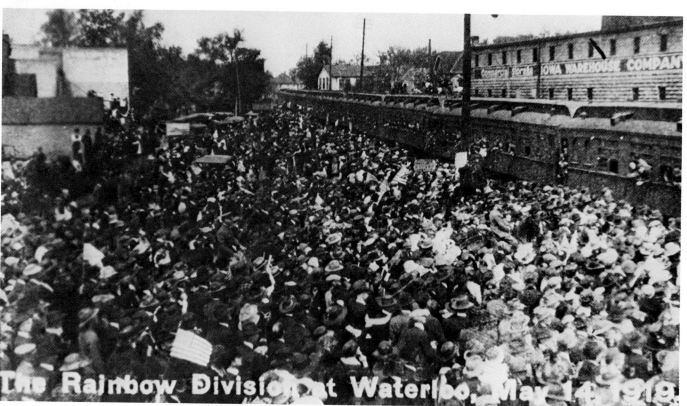

The Rainbow Division at Waterloo, May 14, 1919.

Paul Davis moved his dry goods business to this store on
Commercial Street after the Russell-Lamson Building burned in
1914. Ten years later, when the Caward Brothers put up a new
building on the Russell-Lamson site, Davis moved his store back
and Palace Clothiers took over the Commercial Street store. At the
end of the block, at Commercial and Park, you can see the Flint
Studio sign. Flint was a photographer who worked in Waterloo for
more than forty years and during that period captured on film a
kaleidoscope of the city's life and growth. Directly across Park
Avenue is the Citizens Gas and Electric Company office.
Photo Courtesy of Matt Parrott and Sons Printing Company

125

The Citizens Gas and Electric Company, located on the east side of the river near Rath Packing, was not the first utility service in Waterloo. In 1878, James D. Patton built an artificial gas manufacturing plant between East Park Avenue and East Third Street, a site later occupied by the Illinois Central passenger station. In 1879, C. W. Harvey built a small generator at the west end of the Fourth Street bridge. It provided electricity for some nearby stores and a few streetlights. Ten years later, a Mr. C. D. Jones of Independence, Iowa, acquired both facilities and incorporated the Waterloo Gas and Electric company.

Photo from "Waterloo Way Wins"

Waterloo Gas and Electric changed ownership several times over the years but in 1911, the company was bought by the American Gas Company of Philadelphia and its name was changed to Citizens Gas and Electric. Two years later, the company built their present office building on the corner of Commercial and Park. That same year, they purchased the property where the Maynard Station was later to be built. In 1925, Citizens Gas and Electric merged with two other Iowa utility companies to become Central Iowa Power and Light. More mergers in the next two years created the Iowa Public Service company with headquarters in Sioux City.

Photo Courtesy of Robert Levis

The first source of water for the city was the Cedar River. In 1886, a private company was organized to lay mains and to pump water to homes and businesses. In 1904, after the river water had been declared unfit for use, the company dug the first well in Cedar River Park. The well was deep, going down 1300 feet into the Jordan limestone, and the water was very hard. Three more wells were dug in the park. No one can explain why this particular well has a pagoda style roof. Perhaps its designer believed that a park structure ought to be aesthetic as well as utilitarian.

Photo Courtesy of Waterloo Water Works

Good water in an aquifer about 90 feet down was discovered in the Cedar Bend area so a fifth well was drilled down to that level in 1923. The water was of better quality, less hard than the water from the earlier deep wells which eventually were shut down, removed or used for other purposes. For example, the pagoda, for a number of years, served as a public lavatory.

Photo Courtesy of Waterloo Water Works

The Water Works pump house is located on the east riverbank just north of the Park Avenue Bridge. It stood between the Illinois Central freight house and the passenger station. Those two buildings are gone as are the railroad tracks. The building pictured was torn down in 1935 and a new pump house erected over the steam pumps. In those days, the exhaust steam was funnelled off to heat the Water Works office, the Illinois Central buildings and most of the warehouses along Sycamore Street. The steam was also used to heat the pullman cars waiting at the station to be attached to the late train.

Photo Courtesy of the Waterloo Water Works

This view of east Waterloo was taken during the twenties. Black's Building, the First National Bank, the courthouse, along with a water tower located on the Cutler Hardware Company dominate the skyline. The mills are gone and the appearance of the riverbanks has been improved with a retaining wall. You can barely make out the sign on the Waterloo Fruit and Commission Company's warehouse and the refrigerator freight cars on the siding. At the far left is the Maynard Power station which was completed in 1918 with a capacity of 10,000 kilowatts. Demand for electricity continued to grow and by 1923, a new generator was added doubling the station's original capacity.
Photo Courtesy of Matt Parrott and Sons Printing Company

In this panoramic view, the long building on the left is the Illinois Central freight house. The next building is the Water Works pump house and beyond that, the passenger station. The cars waiting on the tracks would be linked up to a late night train. On the riverbank in front of the station, you can make out the Jacobsen boat livery.
Photo Courtesy of Matt Parrott and Sons Printing Company

In 1924, The W.C.F. & N. elected to expand services by operating buses to towns not served by the interurbans. Drivers and their vehicles assembled at the terminal building to mark the occasion with this photograph. In their riding pants and puttees, they were a snappy looking outfit. The rural service, however, lasted only six years as the company sold the routes to another bus line.

Photo Courtesy of Robert Levis

The Cedar River has always been a source of recreation. From 1927 to 1933 Jacob Jacobsen owned and operated this boat livery on the east bank of the Cedar. Canoes, rowboats and motor boats were rented to fishermen and pleasure seekers. Mr. Jacobsen died in 1933 and his widow continued operations for another year. Today the east end of Park Avenue Bridge occupies the site. The tall building in the center is the former President Hotel now known as Park Towers, an apartment complex for the elderly. The dark building to the right was a small hotel where the Jacobsen family stayed when they moved to Waterloo in 1918. This is part of the National Bank location.

Photo Courtesy of Mrs. Al Gregersen

By 1910, the WCF&N had an interurban line going north through Denver to Waverly and in 1914, a line going south to Cedar Rapids. From 1914 to 1919, they ran two car trains such as the one shown in the picture to Cedar Rapids. Since the electric line made connections with the steam trains, it was thought the trolley should provide a luxury service such as the passengers were accustomed to find on the regular trains. These interurban cars had open observation platforms, individual seats comfortably upholstered, and a porter on duty who served meals. Midwestern train travellers on this Cedar Rapids run well remember the posh, Pullman like cars that were "fast as bullets," travelling at 90 mph, making the Waterloo-Cedar Rapids run in 90 minutes, with eight stops. The service, however, did not pay off and after 1919, single interurbans made the run, the last one being on February 26, 1956 with George Patty as motorman.

Photo Courtesy of Don Durchenwald

Urban man has always sought out places to socialize. When the saloons closed during prohibition, the men frequented the barber shops and cigar stores. The only cigar store still in business in downtown Waterloo is the National which opened in 1917 on the corner of Sycamore and Fifth. While the store has moved several times, it has always relocated in the same neighborhood. This 1920 photo on the Sycamore corner has a crowd clustered at the window. Hard to say why. Perhaps the proprietor has just posted the World Series scores for the day.

Photo Courtesy of Robert Levis

Shores Fuel and Transfer Company is a stock example of how a business changes over the years. They began as a coal and coke selling business. Then they added a draying service, promising to move anything any size — safes, pianos, etc. In later years, their "real service" changed over to warehousing and providing storage space. Their first trucks closely resembled their old horse drawn equipment.

Photo Courtesy of Don Durchenwald

Fuel and Transfer Company
- - - Office, 1209 East 4th Street

All critical housekeepers insist on having their goods fresh, proclaimed the Home Tea Store at 110 E. Fourth street and they promised to deliver just that to their customers — the finest of teas and coffee roasted fresh daily. Like the Great Atlantic and Pacific Tea Company of the era, theirs was a specialty shop and not a grocery store. In addition to tea and coffee, the firm boasted fine spices, extracts, baking powder and a few staples. This shop appears to have sold crockery, as well.

Photo Courtesy of Don Durchenwald

The Taylor Music Store, "the leading music house of Northern Iowa" was one of seven such stores in the city which sold pianos, instruments and sheet music. The piano was the chief source of home entertainment and every family strived to own one. The Victrola had not yet caught on and radio was part of future progress.

Photo from Black Hawk County Atlas, 1910

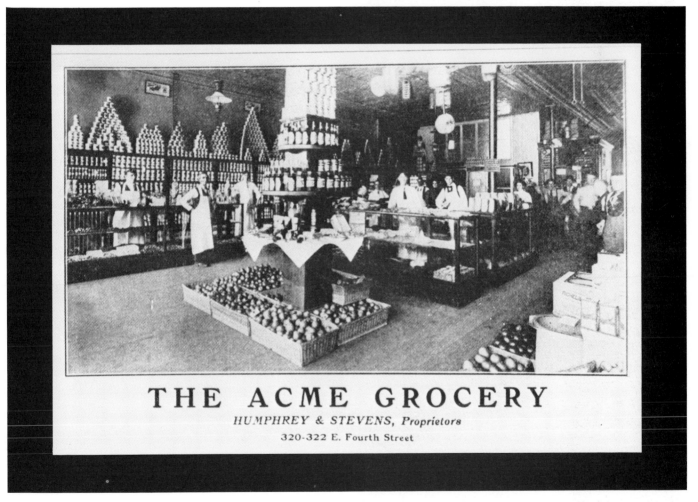

THE ACME GROCERY
HUMPHREY & STEVENS, Proprietors
320-322 E. Fourth Street

Up until World War II, there were a host of grocery stores in the downtown area and the majority of them made home deliveries. The Acme at 320 Fourth Street offered a full line of staple and fancy goods and employed eight clerks to give the customer "polite attention" and full satisfaction. In the picture, the produce department seems to consist wholly of apples. To qualify as an Acme clerk, you had to become adept at using a long pole to knock the topmost can down from the pyramidal displays on the high shelves, as well as being nimble fingered enough to catch it with your other hand. No customer would buy dented cans of fruit.

Photo from Black Hawk County Atlas, 1910

During the twenties, movies were the most popular form of entertainment. Waterloo residents patronized at least seven theaters at any given time. There was the Majestic (always a clean show), the Columbia, Waterloo, the Strand, State, Orpheum and the Rialto. The most sumptuous, the true picture palace, symbolic of the great age of movie making, was the Riviera, later renamed the Paramount. Constructed in 1927, it dominated the east end of the Fourth Street Bridge across from J. C. Penney's, now the National Bank site. Its exterior suggested an Italian palace while its auditorium gave the illusion of being a walled garden. Clouds floated overhead and stars twinkled in the ceiling. It had thick carpeting, wide staircases, and, most welcome on hot days — air conditioning. The theater was also designed for stage plays but the one drawback was its location next to the Illinois Central belt line. The huffing and chuffing of engines sometimes drowned out an actor's most dramatic lines. People quit going to the movies and, in 1972, the Paramount was demolished as part of the downtown flood control project.

Photo Courtesy of Earl Freshwater

During the thirties, you could go dancing at the Electric Park Ballroom beneath its glittering ceiling ball or you could cross the street to Johnson's Gardens and dance the night away to the music of Spider Kurth's Orchestra. Walter Kurth got his nickname "Spider" as a teenage professional boxer. The five-foot nine, one hundred and twenty pound boxer lasted five years in the fighting arena. After recovering from a couple of knockouts, he decided it was in his best interest to try another line of work. He took his life savings, entered the University of Iowa, dropped out eighteen months later to become Spider Kurth.

Photo Courtesy of Mrs. Hubert LaPole

Around 1920, the W.C.F. & N. utilized this type of car, a smaller version of their big interurbans for their Cedar Falls run. The sign on the front of the car is for the benefit of visitors to Waterloo attending the Dairy Cattle Congress.

Photo Courtesy of Robert Levis

A major windstorm struck the dairy show grounds leveling three of the frame barns in September, 1925, just three days before opening day. The enterprising John G. Miller, Waterloo building contractor, rounded up every available carpenter, bricklayer, and mason he could find and set to work rebuilding. They made it in time for the opening day ceremonies. Today, all the cattle barns are made of brick.

Photo Courtesy of National Cattle Congress Fair

This aerial view of the Dairy Show was probably taken in the early thirties. The street is Rainbow Drive and the large building is the hippodrome, renamed McElroy Auditorium. The cattle barns are the long narrow buildings in the foreground while the two white pavilions were used for commercial exhibits. The tents beyond the hippodrome housed farm machinery displays. Beyond the tents was the area reserved for carnival shows. Directly behind that, Electric Park can be identified by the curved roof of the ballroom and at the treeline is the spire tower of the airplane ride. The main gate where spectators lined up to purchase tickets was located at the corner of Rainbow Drive and Westfield Avenue. The spherical object at the far right of the picture was a gas storage tank owned by IPS (Illinois Public Service).
Photo Courtesy of National Cattle Congress Fair

©FARM RECORDS CO., WATERLOO, IOWA
DAIRY CATTLE CONGRESS   1936.
PARADE OF CHAMPION CATTLE

For many years the show in the hippodrome always opened with a parade of the prize winning cattle. The parade and announcements and awards took up most of the show time with vaudeville acts, acrobats or trained dogs following the "main event" parade. Today, beneath the streamers, it is Willie Nelson, the Beach Boys or Barnes Rodeo that take the spotlight. When the entertainers have finished, depending on how long the program is, there may be a showing of some saddle horses. Things do change.

Photo Courtesy of National Cattle Congress Fair

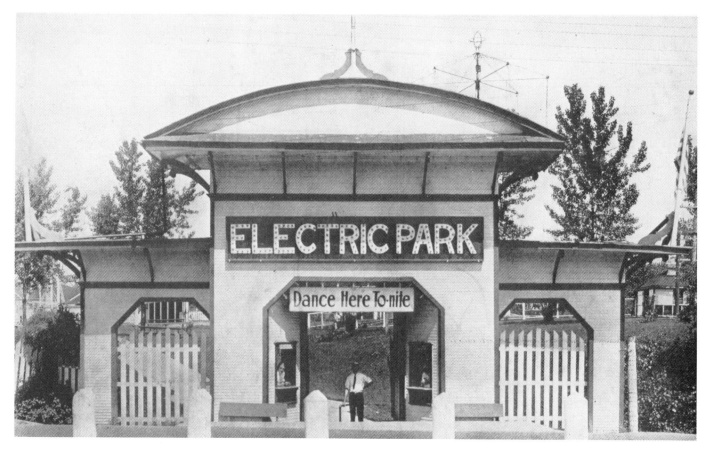

The name was Electric Park and it was spelled out in bright, electric lights. There was fun for kids of all ages: you could see an old-time movie, ride the Spiral Thriller, or dance the night away. Although the park was located some distance from the center of town, it was easy to get there on the streetcar. In fact, the Waterloo, Cedar Falls and Northern, created a subsidiary company to build the Electric Park.

Photo Courtesy of Robert Levis

The management of Electric Park tried different attractions to lure crowds out to the park. As boxing matches with paid admission are illegal in Iowa, free fights were staged along with other athletic events on Wednesday evenings. Clubs or organizations that opted to hold picnics in the park were served urns of coffee free of charge. Judging by the crowd below, the management's efforts met with success.

Photo Courtesy of Robert Levis

The Barrel of Fun was always popular and not nearly as scary as the roller coaster. On "Kid's Day," in the amusement park, rides were just a nickel and ice cream cones cost two cents. (What kid could pass that up?) Today nothing remains of Electric Park but the name and the ballroom where once the big bands played long into the summer's night.

Photo Courtesy of Robert Levis

The entertainment went "up and down" over the years but undoubtedly the most exciting ride was the Spiral Thriller roller coaster. Waterloo boasted, with justification, that it had the best amusement park in the Midwest.

Photo Courtesy of Robert Levis

Around 1907, real estate developers Lewis Lichty and John Steely began selling home sites in an area that was to become Waterloo's most prestigious residential district. Bounded by Independence on the south, Steely on the west, Idaho, east, and Vine to the north, Highland displays some of the most outstanding homes, architecturally, in the city. Several were designed by Mortimer Cleveland, an architect of Waterloo schools and public buildings. Some of the city's most prominent citizens lived in Highland: John and Reuben Rath, both presidents of Rath Packing; Keith Funston, later president of the New York Stock Exchange; A. B. Chambers, later day mayor of Des Moines. Bordered by railroads which impeded expansion, Highland has been able to retain its character as a unique neighborhood. The Highland Neighborhood Association publishes a newsletter and a directory and its activities help maintain the spirit of the community. The photo shows Alta Vista Avenue, one of the main east-west streets in the Highland area. The large house with the colonnades belonged to Frank Eighmey. The other street at right angles to Alta Vista is Highland Boulevard.

Photo Courtesy of Sue Pearson

The two homes shown here are considered some of the finest examples of architecture in northeast Iowa. Both were designed by Mortimer Cleveland. The house with the gambrel roof was built by Ben Lichty at 205 Prospect Avenue in 1909. Claud Cass, one of the owners of the Waterloo, Cedar Falls and Northern Railway, lived here for thirty-seven years. During the sixties the residence became the convent for the nuns who taught at St. John's School. The other home at 215 Prospect was built by Cleveland as his own home. Members of his family still reside there.

Photo Courtesy of Mrs. Dorothy Cleveland

Prohibition, the great experiment, was no more successful in Waterloo than in other parts of the country. Malt was a big seller in the grocery stores as some people made home brew or wine while others built stills like the one shown in the picture. Bootlegging was a booming business.

The 18th Amendment, passed in 1919 and reinforced with the Volstead Act, came as the culmination of over half century of lobbying by temperance groups. Its passage was supported by businessmen who thought the abolition of saloons would create a more efficient and sober working class. World War I had demonstrated the importance of conserving grain but anyone with a dollar could find liquor and bootlegging became a major industry more often that not controlled by mobs such as Al Capone's in Chicago. In June of 1931, the *Waterloo Courier* reported the Waterloo arrest of 10 men believed to be connected with the Capone gang. In 1933, the Amendment was repealed. Waterloo and the nation were wet once again.

Photo Courtesy of Waterloo Public Library

The photograph shows workmen laying track on Lafayette Street for the Linden trolley line which went out Lafayette, up Mulberry, terminating at Lafayette and Colorado. The lines on the east side were the Litchfield to the Litchfield factory, the Highland to St. Francis Hospital, and the Cottage which went as far as Beech and Newell. The west side had the Home Park, travelling out to Byrnes Park and the West Ninth ended at Hammond and Forest. There was, of course, a line to Sans Souci which would become part of a loop making a circle from downtown Waterloo, around through Westfield and back to the town center.

Photo Courtesy of Don Durchenwald

During the 1920s, home refrigeration was usually a block of ice delivered by horse and wagon. A card placed in a convenient window told the ice wagon driver how much the lady of the house needed that day — 25, 50, 75 or even 100 pounds, depending on the size of her ice chest. The driver chipped off a chunk, weighed it up and carried it in on his back, using huge tongs. Some homes had built-in ice boxes with doors opening to the outside so the driver did not have to carry his heavy load inside. On hot days, the neighborhood children eagerly followed the "Pied Piper" with ice down the street. If the driver was in a good mood, he might chip a piece of the ice block off and give it to them.

Photo Courtesy of Waterloo Library Collection

Livingston National Air Race Winner

Photo Courtesy Waterloo Public Library

The life of John Livingston, a racing pilot in the twenties and thirties, inspired the novel *Jonathan Livingston Seagull* by Richard Bach and was also made into a movie. Born in Cedar Falls in 1897, he was a flying ace in World War I. He entered 39 air races in the years 1928-1931 and won the 1928 transcontinental air race New York to Los Angeles. He took 9 of 12 first places in the Cleveland Air Races in 1932. He and his brother operated a flying service at Livingston Field (formerly Chapman Field). His death came swiftly and suddenly one day while flight testing a light plane.

Photo Courtesy Waterloo Public Library

Chapman Field, Waterloo's first airport, was dedicated on October 13, 1928. But the first airplane flight into Waterloo occurred some years earlier when Lieutenant Milo Miller flew his plane from his base in Texas to Waterloo to visit his parents, landing in Byrnes Park. After WWI, he and George Searles leased land from the park, and with three old army trainers, started a flying service, offering 10 minute rides over the city for ten dollars. John Livingston worked for them as a mechanic. Perry Canfield, lumberman, and Fisher Marshall, automobile dealer, built private airstrips which were used by barnstormers. A meeting of concerned businessmen on July 12, 1927 set the scene for the development of a city airport. The chief speaker declared that the future growth of Waterloo would be determined, in large measure, by its airport facilities. A. B. Chambers, later a mayor of Des Moines, was appointed chairman in charge of raising funds. At the $50,000 mark, the corporation bought 120 acres of land east of Waterloo on old highway 20, named it Chapman Field and leased it to Midwest Airways Corporation who initiated plane service to Des Moines. After 11 months, the service closed down for lack of business. John and Alden Livingston leased the field and provided pilot training, charter and recreational service. In 1942, they bought the field and set up a flight instructional base for the army. In 1943, the U.S. government approved a grant for the construction of a municipal airport.

The young men in the picture are two student pilots at Chapman Field in 1928 with their instructor John Cable who became a test pilot at Lockheed.

Photo Courtesy Waterloo Public Library

Chapman Field Training for Student

The workers building East High School in 1919 got a welcome break while the photographer took a picture of the work in progress. The school, designed by Mortimer Cleveland, was not the first high school on the corner of High and Vine Streets. The first east side secondary school, built here in 1874, became Hawthorne Elementary when a new high school was built on the corner of Mulberry and Fifth. Hawthorne burned in 1915 so the board of education decided to build a new high school on that site and turn the school on Mulberry into the city's first junior high school. The school at High and Vine remains as East High School but the school on Mulberry is now the site of Waterloo's city hall. In 1921, another elementary school was built on Franklin and named Hawthorne. Today it houses the Expo alternative school, a program for children who do not function well in the usual classroom setting.

Photo Courtesy of Mrs. Dorothy Cleveland

Golf first came on the Waterloo scene on Sans Souci Island in 1900 when 20 people organized a golf clubhouse and built a nine hole course. The course was battered by frequent flooding and in the last year of its existence (1908) had only five holes. Byrnes Park golf course was started in 1906 and was leased to the Waterloo Golf and Country club in 1908. In 1914, it became a municipal course where it cost 10 cents to play a round or twenty-five cents to play all day. In 1919, a new golf organization purchased the Sunnyside Farm from George Lichty and F. J. Fowler and created Sunnyside Country Club. By 1920, an eighteen hole course had been constructed covering 160 acres. The club was financed by selling shares at $100 to 250 members with George Lichty as the first president.
Photo Courtesy of Don Durchenwald

Michael McElroy, the popular host of a "man-on-the-street" talk show originally came to Waterloo as a salesman for WMT radio station in 1935. He pole-vaulted to radio stardom with his "Voice of Iowa" program sponsored by Altstadt and Langlas Bakery, makers of Kleen Maid Bread. Aired daily 12:20 to 12:30, except Sunday, "hundreds of thousands" of listeners tuned in to "Mac, the the most curious man in the world"—the Paul Harvey of yesteryear. When WMT closed its Waterloo studio, then located in the Russell Lamson Hotel, McElroy became part of the new Black Hawk Broadcasting Company whose station call letters were KWWL.
Photo Courtesy of Altstadt and Langlas Bakery

Interior of old Sunnyside Golf Clubhouse.
Photo Courtesy of Mrs. Dorothy Cleveland

Hogs usually arrived at the Rath plant by truck and immediately checked into the "Hog Hotel," the large 4-story, slatted building in the center of the picture. The hotel's cold showers kept them comfortable in hot weather. Refrigerated rail cars carried the finished products off to market. At one time, a phenomenal 35 carloads of Rath products were shipped out daily. Today, refrigerated trucks move the hams and bacon to stores and distributors.

Photo Courtesy of Rath Packing Company

The Rath name is associated with hams and bacon but Rath's also bought cattle and supplied fresh beef to shops and restaurants. After the war, the beef kill was discontinued at the Waterloo plant and the company bought dressed carcasses from other packers. Lamb, popular and plentiful, was also processed at Rath's. The company kept a holding area for sheep on Highway 20 East outside of town. This picture of busy beef cutters at work was taken by Flint in 1938.

Photo Courtesy of Rath Packing Company

By 1940, Rath's had over 5000 employees and killed more animals than any packing plant in the nation. It was said that more hogs were killed in Waterloo than any other place in the world. By 1952, the number of employees had grown to 6500 and the Rath empire expanded with plants in Columbus Junction, Iowa, Houston and San Antonio, Texas and Birmingham, Alabama. Like most of the nation's older packing plants in the 70's, Rath's was in trouble and experiencing financial reverses. To keep the company alive, the employees in 1979, voted to purchase stock with part of their earnings. Rath employees are now represented on the board of directors and have a voice in matters that affect their work.

Photo Courtesy of Rath Packing Company

145

Gasoline cost less than 70 cents a gallon when the Northland stations were operating in Waterloo. This one was located on West Fifth Street where Conway Inne now stands. Northland had several stations located in different parts of the city but the war years were difficult and challenging times for the gasoline business. It was hard to keep employees who regularly defected to better paying jobs in factories with armed services contracts. As an added hardship, gasoline was rationed to both dealers and consumers. Northland got out of the service station business, but it continues to this day to sell other petroleum products.
· Note the old style pump between the more modern ones.
Photo Courtesy of Ron Lompe

Hubert LaPole operated his newsstand until forced to close it down in 1946. Most of the magazines shown here were once popular publications. How many do you recognize and remember?

Photo Courtesy of Mrs. Hubert LaPole

Hubert LaPole who owned this newsstand on the corner of Sycamore and Fourth Streets sold newspapers and magazines here for more than 60 years. He began working at age eleven to help support his family. He would get up at three A.M., collect the *Chicago Tribune* and sell until time to go to school. At noon he was out selling the early edition of the *Waterloo Courier* and, after school, he sold the evening edition. When a local store owner declared the newsstand a nuisance and tried to get rid of it, LaPole took the case to the Iowa Supreme Court. He lost and was forced to give up the stand but he continued to sell papers on the same corner. When Fourth Street was in the process of renovation, he moved to the corner of Fifth and Sycamore and remained there until his death in 1983.

Photo Courtesy of Mrs. Hubert LaPole

In 1931, the West Side School System opened Lowell Elementary School, of which it was said that, "The beauty of its exterior architecture and the lovely color harmonies of the interior are a part of the daily inspiration of 760 children." The large school, surrounded by extensive grounds, has spacious halls with tiled walls. The unique lobby has a small fountain and the ceiling is decorated with frescoes. The gym with its large stage can double as an auditorium. There is also a little theater and a specially designed science room. The cafeteria in the basement is now used as a library. When Lowell was built, the public library provided library service one day a week.
Photo from Pictorial Review of West Waterloo Schools, 1933-34

"The kindergarten provides the first steps in working together — the highest type of social relationship." One of the most attractive rooms at Lowell is the kindergarten. The windows are large and low to allow small heads to peek out. A most unusual feature, for a classroom, is the fireplace. A tile frieze near the ceiling depicts characters from nursery stories and rhymes. Out of sight of the camera is a tile fish pool. This photo was taken in 1933.
Photo from Pictorial Review of West Waterloo Schools, 1933-34

When Saint Mary's parish moved out of the downtown, the old school became the home of the *Waterloo Morning Tribune*. Isaiah Van Metre founded the *Tribune* in 1879 and merged it with the *Waterloo Times* in 1901. William Reed became the editor in 1907. He bought WJAM, a station in Cedar Rapids and began broadcasting from both cities with the call letters, WMT. In 1931, Reed sold his newspaper to the *Waterloo Courier*. The Reed family continued to run the Tribune Press, a job printing business, continuing to work out of the old schoolhouse. When the press was moved to new quarters on Falls Avenue, the school was torn down and the site is now the parking lot for the YWCA.

Photo Courtesy of Don Durchenwald

It wasn't quite like a real train but it meant sheer delight to an era of Waterloo youngsters. The Illinois Central created this miniature train for use in parades and special events. It was made in the Illinois Central shops where the workmen built the big engines. This charming replica boasted an engine, freight car, cattle car and, naturally, a caboose. In this picture, taken in front of East High School, the children apparently think the coal tender is the best place to ride.

Photo Courtesy of Robert Levis

The most lucrative part of the Waterloo, Cedar Falls and Northern operation was the freight and switching service. It had a belt line that connected with most of the factory districts on both sides of the river and with its interchanges it could move freight cars for all three railroads. It shared the switching at Rath's with the Illinois Central and did all the switching for John Deere. When the WCF&N went out of business, the Illinois Central and the Rock Island organized the Waterloo Railroad to take over the switching and freight business. Today, with the Rock Island gone by the wayside, the Illinois Central has charge over all the switching once performed by the WCF&N.

Photo Courtesy of Robert Levis

After the buses replaced the trolley cars, the WCF&N continued to run an electric interurban to Cedar Falls. When this service closed down in 1958, it was the last known trolley car to run in Iowa. The trolley in this picture was placed in Cedar River Park until vandalism almost destroyed it. It was repaired in the railway shops in Charles City and then taken to the Old Threshers Museum in Mt. Pleasant, Iowa. There, on a track on the museum grounds, it brings to life for the new generation of children what it was like to ride on the trolley car.

Photo Courtesy of Robert Levis

The hemlines look 1980 rather than 1928 when this photo was snapped of Black's Millinery Department. The flapper hats, the seductive bonnet of the "Roaring Twenties," can be seen on the counter at right. Melba Durchenwald, wife of local historian and engineer, Don, came to work in this department the fateful year of 1929 when the Roaring Twenties' bubble burst.

Photo Courtesy of Melba Durchenwald

Longfellow school was built in 1940 with WPA funds. It replaced three other older schools — Louisa Alcott, John Fisk and Washington. The first two schools were torn down. Washington School was, until 1966, the home of the city's recreational program. Longfellow is a very large building with plenty of playground space. The spacious, bright classrooms housed a small adjacent office for the teacher's use. The school also has a large gym, a little theater, art room and a library. Because of the size of the facility, the school has, at times, housed rooms for the hearing impaired, brain damaged children and several classrooms for the mentally retarded.

Photo Courtesy of Waterloo Community Schools

The first Bishop's Cafeteria in the Midwest was established in Waterloo in 1920 by Benjamin Franklin Bishop who was born on September 10, 1873 at Brush Creek, Iowa and died on March 24, 1928 in Waterloo. Initially working in the hotel industry, he managed cafeterias in West Des Moines, Sioux City and Cedar Rapids before selecting Waterloo as the site of his own cafeteria. Bishop, an aesthetic man, was also a poet, artist and photographer. He had great fun putting on his annual Christmas dinner for the Waterloo newsboys. Ben Bishop once said that he lost a lot of his children when they became teens but always gained them back in the fold when they married and started bringing in their own children. This billboard advertises his cafeteria at an east and west location.

Photo Courtesy of Robert Levis

CHAPTER IV

1940 - Present

Everyone remembers what he or she was doing the moment it was announced that Pearl Harbor had been bombed. It was a tense moment in our history; finally, the waiting was over. America was at war.

On the home front, people learned to put up with the rationing of gasoline, tires and food stuffs. Women did without sugar, meat and butter in the preparation of meals, and, taking a step back in time, they gardened and canned their own produce. Shoes, too, were rationed and restrictions were placed on the manufacturing of clothing. Dresses were short and cuffs disappeared from men's pants. To save on gas, people drove at 35 miles per hour and bought retreaded tires. They walked more, drove less and took the bus. Women, liberated from the home, took over as factory workers in the absence of America's male work force.

Most factories had defense contracts. Chamberlains, once the number one manufacturer of washing machine wringers, made shell casings. John Deere manufactured tank parts. During the never ending depression decade, there hadn't been much money to buy consumer goods. Now, everybody was working and had money but there was nothing much to buy.

Victory in Japan day. No one could quite grasp the horror of the atomic bomb; America simply rejoiced because the war was over. The wartime economy took a slow turn towards a peacetime economy. No cars had been produced during the war and everyone needed a new one. No houses had been built and the number one priority of returning veterans was to house their families. People lived in anything vaguely resembling shelter — garages, renovated chicken coops. They built basements, put roofs over their heads and waited until the shortage of building materials eased. It was a time of frustration but it was a time of hope. Things would, of course, get better.

During the fifties, downtown Waterloo was a bustling center; the major challenge, however, was finding a place to park. The city built two parking ramps, one on each side of the river which relieved congestion slightly. The many downtown grocery stores disappeared to be replaced by supermarkets at the edge of the business district or out in the residential areas. The shopping plaza era had made its debut.

Highway 218 between Waterloo and Cedar Falls was relocated and made into a four-lane. Numerous businesses set up shop alongside the thoroughfare. Waterloo and Cedar Falls had once been seven miles apart with farm land in between. Now they were rubbing shoulders. The exodus of stores from the downtown to areas where there was plenty of parking had begun. No one quite realized at the time what that would eventually mean to the city.

During the sixties, Waterloo replaced two major public buildings, the city hall and the courthouse. The old city hall had been inadequate for fifty years. Most of the city departments were located in the Lafayette Building next door and there was a walkway over the alley between the two structures. The raising of two new junior high schools on the east side left the old junior high at Mulberry and Fifth available. The city purchased the property and finally erected a city hall everyone could be proud of. Meanwhile, the county discovered the courthouse on Park Avenue was falling apart at the seams and could not be repaired. The Board of Supervisors bought the block on Fifth between Mulberry and Lafayette in the hopes the new edifice could house all county departments. However, after a few short years the Social Services department was forced to find larger quarters elsewhere.

The railroad dropped passenger service and a problem that had long plagued Waterloo began to dissipate. Traffic had often been backed up for blocks because of the downtown crossings. The Illinois Central removed its passenger station and parts of the beltline that crossed Fifth, Fourth and Park Avenues. With the demise of the Rock Island, the only line left to stop traffic was the Northwestern.

The seventies saw the death of the downtown as the major shopping area. Two shopping malls in the metropolitan area plus other retail centers attracted the buying public now accustomed to driving their own vehicles in preference to riding the bus. J. C. Penney, Sears and Montgomery Ward all moved out of the downtown area with other retailers following. The climate controlled malls with ample parking space offered shopping ease. Even though the local economy was good, downtown Waterloo resembled a ghost town. The downtown merchants fought back by making Fourth Street more attractive, planting trees and encouraging the remaining businesses to improve the appearance of their stores.

The physical appearance of the city changed tremendously during this period. On the west side, Conway Convention Center was built on the block once dotted with small stores and dominated by the Black Hawk Bank Building. Across Fourth Street, the former J. C. Penney Store has been supplanted by a high-rise attractive hotel. The old Waterloo Savings Bank Building is still there on Commercial but the stores on either side have disappeared. Fourth Street now curves gently toward the bridge. There is a new parking garage next to the old one. Skywalks lead hotel patrons to the garage or convention center.

Fifth and Fourth Street bridges as well as Sans Souci bridge were replaced after the war. A new bridge was built at First Street and another planned for Sixth. A system of one-way streets moves traffic efficiently about town.

One sometimes wonders what kind of city Mary Hanna envisioned when she stood on the banks of the Cedar River in 1845. In 1980, Waterloo had a population of over 75,000. Not a big city by modern standards but bigger than any city Mary Hanna ever dreamed of. Today, she would be pleased by Waterloo's 114 churches and 28 public schools. She would, doubtless, enjoy the outdoors in our 78 public parks but maybe question how people find the time to chase little balls around a golf or tennis court. She would fall in love with the Waterloo Public Library and, perhaps, find the architecture of the city's public buildings impressive but not quite grand enough for her Victorian taste. In her day, she bore witness to the advent of the railroads and the early beginnings of the city's industrial age. She would have been proud of the enterprising Waterloo of 1910 with its 150 factories employing 7,000 workers and utterly amazed that, in 1983, there would be 73 plants employing 20,000. It would boggle her mind to image a factory the size and magnitude of John Deere with 15,000 workers or even Rath's with 2,000. Automobiles were brash newcomers to her landscape in her old age and airplanes were still part of another generation. Could she conceive of an era when horses would be permanently put out to pasture and when Black Hawk County alone would register 108,000 automobiles?

Whatever Mary Hanna had in mind, this is Waterloo, a fine city, our home, a special place along the Cedar River, born and bred from the formidable love and determination of this remarkable woman and nurtured by others of comparable character and aspirations.

Waterloo's depression problems were somewhat alleviated by different federal programs. WPA workers repaired streets and sidewalks and improved the parks. One major project that benefited the city was the Park Avenue Bridge. The original town planners had expected Park Avenue to be the main thoroughfare through the city but no bridge was ever built on that site until 1939. The bridge, 615 feet long, cost $205,000 and was paid for partly by the Iowa State Highway Commission and partly by WPA funds. It was one of the first bridges in the state to have a median dividing the two lanes of traffic. The ribbon cutting dedication ceremony took place on November 21, 1939.

Photo Courtesy of Waterloo Planning Commission

When the old marble post office was declared inadequate, the Post Office Department tore down the Knights of Pythias building and two residences as well as the old post office to make room for a new facility. While it was being built, the post office moved into temporary quarters on Jefferson Street. When the new structure was finished in 1938, (photo below) besides the space allocated for the post office, it contained a large courtroom, judge's chambers and rooms for officers of the court. The third floor housed the Internal Revenue Service, Social Security, Treasury Department and Justice Department. It was intended that other federal agencies such as army and navy recruiting, agricultural extension office, national bank examiner and federal alcohol tax inspector would also find a home in the new building. Eventually, Internal Revenue Service and Social Security, requiring additional space, moved out of the post office. When Federal Court no longer sat in Waterloo, much of this building was unused. In 1976, the post office moved to a new building on Sycamore and the City of Waterloo bought the old building to remodel into a new library.

Photo Courtesy of A. A. Bengston

The worst tragedy of World War II for a local family occurred when the Cruiser *U.S.S. Juneau* was sunk off Guadalcanal during the battle of the Solomons, November 13, 1942. Five sons of the Thomas Sullivan family died that day. The brothers, Albert, Madison, Joseph, George and Francis had enlisted in the Navy with the provision they would be allowed to serve on the same ship. After their simultaneous deaths, the War Department ruled that no two members of a family were to serve in the same military unit. In their honor, the Navy launched a destroyer, *U.S.S. The Sullivans*, christened by their mother in 1943. In 1964, the city established a park in the neighborhood where the boys grew up. A memorial designed to honor the five brothers and all of America's fighting men who died in the cause of freedom was constructed in the park. It consists of a pentagonal base topped with the bronze shamrock insignia of the *U.S.S. The Sullivans*. Each side of the base contains a bronze plaque inscribed with the name of one of the Sullivan brothers.

Photo Courtesy of Waterloo Park Commission

Waterloo organized a YMCA in 1868 with the first permanent building raised in 1898 on the foundation of one of the old mills near the Fourth Street Bridge. The three story structure with first floor shops was designed to serve both boys and girls. Declared obsolete in 1930, it was demolished to make room for a new structure put on the same site. This building, now called the River Plaza, is entered in the National Register of Historic Places. A fine example of the Art Deco style, it was designed by Mortimer Cleveland and his associate D. B. Toenjes.

Photo Courtesy of Black Hawk County YMCA

At the end of World War II, the Illinois Central Railroad moved quickly to replace its steam power with diesels. One of its innovations was this two car train named the Land O'Corn. It left Waterloo in the morning for Chicago and whisked back in that evening. The motors were located underneath and the engineer's seat in the first car was surrounded by the passengers. After the train had an accident, this type of design was discontinued.

Photo Courtesy of Robert Levis

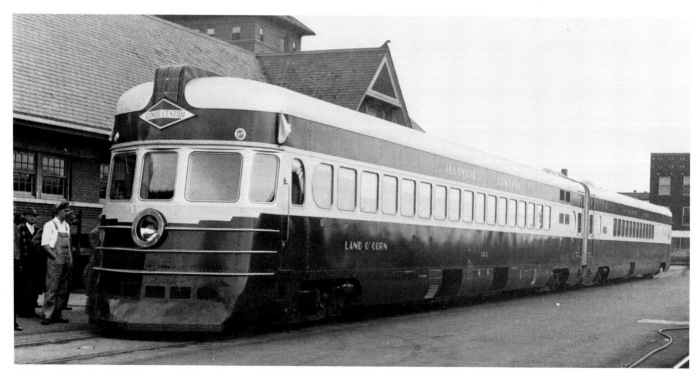

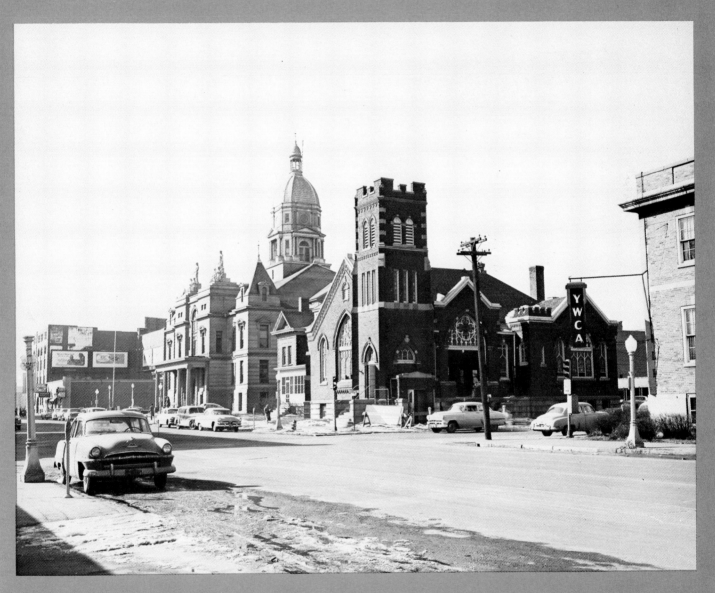

The only building in this photo that has not been torn down is the YWCA. Where the Brethren Church stood on the corner is the present site of Perpetual Savings and Loan. The sheriff's house and the courthouse have become a parking lot. Four of the "green goddess" allegorical statues which graced its roof remain in storage until a suitable location can be found for them. Across Sycamore Street, the stores and warehouses have disappeared and this area, too, has become a haven for parked cars.

Photo Courtesy of the Waterloo Park Department

Walter Betsworth, former airport manager, is shown holding an ear of corn that was one of the crops grown on airport land. The farming operation started in 1947 with local farmers doing the work on a share basis. Today, the maintenance crew farms the land as well as taking care of airport facilities. The crops have remained constant over the years with corn, soybeans, hay, rye, and oats planted on 1600 acres, representing 80% of the land owned by the airport. The income from the farmland has saved the taxpayer's money over the years and continues to be an important source of revenue. In 1943, the city had purchased 1,700 acres and some years later added another 1,000. The farm land has provided a needed buffer zone between the airport and nearby property owners. The supreme court had ruled in favor of residents adjacent to airports who complained about the nuisance noise. Fortunately, the foxes which are seen near the fields and which sometimes frolic on the runways do not complain.

Photo Courtesy of Georgia Betsworth

The original terminal building at the Waterloo Airport was a quonset hut. Construction on the main part of the present terminal was begun in 1949, the tower added in 1958. The present facility is 1,200 square feet larger than the original. February 1, 1948 marked the date of the first flight of Mid-Continent Airlines which flew from Minneapolis to Kansas City, Mo. Several air lines have served the airport — Mid-Continent, Braniff and Ozark. Commuter air lines became popular in the 1970's with Coleman Air, Mississippi Valley, Mid-State, and American Central using the facilities for limited periods of time. American Central and Ozark currently share use of the terminal. Niederhauser Air Lines, a charter service, has occupied hangars since the 1960s. In 1974, Congress mandated that all federally aided and certified airports must have a fire station. One 24 hour fireman is on duty with another man added during flight times. The specially equipped fire truck can pump water at the rate of 1,500 gallons a minute and is also equipped with chemicals and foam designed for fuel fires.

Photo Courtesy of Georgia Betsworth

This aerial picture was taken at the official dedication of the Waterloo Municipal Airport on June 10, 1951. Fifteen hundred cars filled the parking lots and adjacent land. Planning for the facility began in 1937. A special election in 1945 approved the organization of an airport commission. The first airport manager was a Mr. Omdalen. Walter Betsworth replaced him in 1948 and continued in that position until 1972. The configuration of three 5,400 foot runways is the same today as it was in 1951 except for an 8,400 foot runway to accommodate jet planes. The airfield is named Livingston/Betsworth Field after John Livingston, famous local aviator, and Mr. Betsworth.

Photo Courtesy of Waterloo Airport

During the thirties, there were two radio stations broadcasting in Waterloo, WMT with studios in the Russell-Lamson Hotel and KXEL located in the Insurance Building on the corner of Fourth and Franklin. WMT decided to give up their Waterloo studio and broadcast only from Cedar Rapids so the newly organized Black Hawk Broadcasting company under the leadership of Ralph ("Mike") McElroy took over WMT's studio in the hotel and began broadcasting under the letters KWWL. Competition ran high between KXEL and KWWL over which station would obtain the right to TV broadcasting on channel 7. Feeling confident of success, KXEL built a new station out on highway 20, but it was KWWL that was granted the rights. For some years, they shared KXEL's studio out on the highway; eventually, they found it more convenient to combine their radio and television functions in the Insurance Building. Television did not kill off radio. The two stations have grown to ten in the Waterloo-Cedar Falls area.

Photo Courtesy of Helen Hoy

Jesse Cosby Neighborhood Center is located at 1112 Mobile Street in the old St. Peter Claver Catholic Church. Founded in 1966, the facility added a senior citizen center in 1978. The primary purpose of the center is to initiate and encourage programs and activities which serve the needs and desires of the people in East Waterloo, Evansdale and Elk Run. It provides services such as helping individuals fill out application forms, counselling for careers and education, home management and leisure time. Courses are given in adult basic education, crafts, money management, parenting and physical fitness. There is a special program for senior citizens in health, crafts, and consumer education. The center is one of the noon hot meal sites sponsored by the Hawkeye Valley Area Agency on Aging.
Photo Courtesy of Helen Hoy

Jesse Cosby, for whom the center is named, lived in Waterloo for only 12 years but in that interval endeared himself to many for his musical talents and leadership abilities. Born in Jefferson County, Alabama, in 1907, he was employed at the Waterloo Recreation Center, was an UNI instructor and a participant in the White House Conference on Children and Youth. Cosby organized the first black A Capella choir in the city.
Photo Courtesy of Jesse Cosby Center

One of Jesse Cosby's special talents was square dance calling. He was often invited to participate at national square dance schools and festivals.

Photo Courtesy of Jesse Cosby Center

The old West High School on West Fifth Street had been, from its inception, a 6-year school, combining both junior and senior high schools. When a new senior high was built on the corner of Ridgeway and Baltimore in 1955, West High became West Junior High. Sloane Wallace Junior High, which had been created out of two old schools, was consequently torn down. Population growth in Waterloo, favoring the west and south sides of the city, soon had the new senior high straining at the seams, so new classrooms were added. A new junior high, Hoover, was also built not too far from the new West High.

Photo Courtesy of the Waterloo Community Schools

In the fifties, you could still take a passenger train from the Rock Island Station on Bluff Street going to either Kansas City or Minneapolis or climb aboard a Great Western train from this same station heading for Chicago or Des Moines. During the sixties, the passenger trains all but disappeared and a whole generation has grown up without ever learning the finer points of dressing and undressing in an upper berth. This depot is the only remaining passenger station in the city.

Photo Courtesy of Robert Levis

The opening event of Centennial Week was a race between a 1909 Maytag auto and a steam engine. The Rock Island provided the engine plus several cars and a caboose. The engine was a 10-4 model with a diamond stack. The car was owned and driven by antique auto collector, Harry Burd. He and his passenger, Fran Allison, radio and TV star, ("Kukla, Fran and Ollie") are dressed in dusters and goggles appropriate for a drive in the dusty days of 1900. The race course was run along Bluff Street with 5,000 gathered to cheer on the racers. Because of people crowding up to the track, the engineer was forced to slow down and, with an extra burst of speed, the Maytag was first to cross the finish line.
Photo Courtesy of Waterloo Public Library

Waterloo marked its 1954 centennial year with a week of celebration, highlighted by daily parades, special events and a pageant presented each night reenacting pioneer days. Many people joined in the spirit of the festivities by dressing in buckskin and calico or letting their beards grow. The Prairie Drama, with a cast of 1250, played nightly in the municipal auditorium on the cattle congress grounds.
Photo Courtesy of Waterloo Public Library

The family of Honorable Henry Grout, for whom the Grout Museum of History and Science (photo below) is named, were farmers who came to the Waterloo area in 1858. Henry attended school in the once rural stone schoolhouse now located on Parker Street. He also attended the Field Seminary. As a young man, he went westward "to better his condition" and worked for mines and railroads. After his father's death, he returned to the area and was, alternately, a farmer, realtor and a travelling salesman. He served on the board of directors of the First National Bank, on the city park commission and as a legislator in the 34th and 35th General Assemblies. His hobby was collecting, especially Indian relics and geologic specimens. His will provided for a sum of money to take care of his collection. By 1956, the funds had grown sufficiently to allow the building of the Grout Museum on the corner of South and Park Avenue.

Photo Courtesy of the Grout Museum of History and Science

The museum's first floor, displaying geologic and paleontological specimens as well as Indian artifacts, also houses a small auditorium, library and planetarium. The library holds a collection of historical materials and books on genealogy. Everyone is welcomed here to do research. The planetarium provides weekly shows on astronomy. An antique Maytag auto and a Dart truck, both made in Waterloo, are feature displays on this floor.

Photo Courtesy of the Grout Museum of History and Science

Many of these buildings are still downtown but the businesses have changed. In 1953, the corner housed the Iowa Glass and Paint Company. Today, it belongs to the Waterloo Community Playhouse and is used for costume storage and rental. Around the corner on Water Street, you can make out the sign for Smiley's Hobby shop. Lincoln's Office Supply is now located on East Fourth and Hank's Hardware store is gone. The east side parking ramp takes up the space left by these two stores. Across Fifth Street, the Buick garage has been supplanted by Martin Brothers Distributors.

Photo Courtesy of the Waterloo Park Department

Don Perkins, former running back for the Dallas Cowboys, grew up in Waterloo and graduated from West High School. A halfback on the University of New Mexico team, 1957-1959, he subsequently signed up with the Cowboys, playing professional ball from 1961 to 1968. He was honored as an All-NFL player in 1962. Upon his retirement, his record of 6,217 yards on 1,500 carries, scoring 42 touchdowns, gave him recognition as the fifth greatest rusher in NFL history. He is presently employed by the State Department of Social Services in New Mexico.
Photo Courtesy of Robert Siddens

In 1956, Leonard Katoski of the Park Commission, conceived a dream of twelve "theme" parks where children could "exercise their minds as they exercised their bodies." Over the years, ten such parks have been constructed, bringing nationwide attention to the Waterloo Park system. Few cities have followed such a unique concept. Tibbetts Park, located near the Greenbrier addition, sports a frontier theme. Children can use their imaginations to ward off an Indian attack, chase buffalo across the plains, or burrow into a mining tunnel.
Photo Courtesy of the Waterloo Park Commission

Parents and children may dream of an adventure on a tropical island and Robinson Crusoe Park offers a magical journey for children of all ages. Dredging a channel in the Cedar River created an island that provided the perfect setting for this dream of Leonard Katoski. Park maintenance started work on the project in 1959 and, hopefully, it will never be fully completed. Children climb into the tri-level tree house, take shelter in the native huts, sail Crusoe's ship, "El Rio Cedro," and grill hot dogs over a cannibal's kettle. Although the park was designed with children in mind, the whole family will enjoy the fanciful facilities.

Photo Courtesy of the Waterloo Park Commission

In 1942, when superintendent of schools for the west side Charles Kittrell, suddenly died, it seemed an opportune time to combine the two school systems. The enlarged district, with additional administrative staff and services being offered to teachers, required more space than could be provided in the high schools. Built in 1960, this administration building houses the superintendent's office, board of education, media services, business offices, and consultants' offices. It is located on Washington Street near Lowell School.

Photo Courtesy of Waterloo Community Schools

Anyone who lived in Waterloo in the early fifties should remember this corner with its assortment of cafes, taverns and small shops. Friedl's Coffee Cup was a landmark on the west side for many years. Later, it became Friedl's Prime Rib Room. Most of these businesses were razed to make way for the west side parking ramp. The remaining structures, between the old ramp and the old Waterloo Savings Bank building, were demolished when the 1983 parking ramp went in.

Photo Courtesy of the Waterloo Park Department

Old-timers who can remember the many Waterloo floods describe the 1929 flood as being the worst that ever happened to the city. The flood that overwhelmed us in March of 1961 probably matched 1929. Damage in '61 was estimated at 60 million dollars. The floodwaters reached the highest point ever recorded at the Sixth Street gauge — 21.86 feet. This flood prompted the city to request federal aid for a flood control program.
Photo Courtesy of Waterloo Public Library

Twenty-seven hundred teenagers were among the 4,000 volunteers who worked all night loading sandbags and building dikes to keep the floodwaters from overwhelming the business district. The photo was taken in the Sans Souci area.
Photo Courtesy of Waterloo Public Library

In 1910, consultant Charles Robinson informed the city of Waterloo that a new city hall was in order. Getting its citizens to agree on a location took the next fifty years. In 1935, the city considered Lincoln Park as the site for a new city hall but it was rejected. In 1949, the city fathers also thought of buying and remodeling the Insurance Building on the corner of Fourth and Franklin. In 1951, there was an election for a new city hall with no specific site named. That was turned down. In 1956, the city and the county considered building a composite city-county edifice in Lincoln Park. The citizenry put thumbs down on the idea, too. In 1958, the city held an unofficial ballot asking voters to choose from three sites — Lincoln Park, a proposed civic center site on the west bank of the river, or the old east junior high building at Mulberry and Fifth. The voters selected the junior high and in 1960, a half century late, Waterloo got its new city hall.

Photo Courtesy of Helen Hoy

This more conventional train replaced the first Land O'Corn. Passenger service disappeared from all the railroads in the sixties. The Land O'Corn was one of the last to go. The passenger station, the freight house and the warehouses along Sycamore have all vanished from this section of town. Only the water works pumphouse remains. Cut off from the riverbanks by a flood wall for several years, this area has been a city parking lot. In 1983, an apartment house for retirees was built on a section of the parking lot.

Photo Courtesy of Robert Levis

Byrnes Park was originally laid out as a series of drives through the lovely trees. The Park Authority, established in 1904, built a 9-hole golf course on this west side location in 1908. In 1924, the golf course was expanded to 18-holes, all of which had grass greens as did the original course.

The Byrnes Park area also includes one of the two municipal swimming pools, playground facilities, and 25,000 annual flower plantings. The swimming pool was financed by a bond issue in 1960, then a new pool was built on the site in 1980.

Photo Courtesy of the Waterloo Park Commission

Back in the fifties, courthouse employees found their workplace falling down around their heads. The steel reenforced concrete ceilings were coming apart and supports had to be placed in strategic places. Moreover, several departments had grown to the point they had to be housed in other buildings. The supervisors' first plan was to build an L-shaped building encircling the courthouse. A citizens' committee objected to this arrangement, pointing out that there would be no room for parking. The property bounded by Fifth, Mulberry, Sixth, and Lafayette was available and it was purchased. In 1964, the present courthouse was dedicated. The old courthouse was torn down and the area became a parking lot.

Photo Courtesy of Helen Hoy

The first community playhouse in Iowa was the Waterloo Community Drama League founded in 1916. Their first permanent home was the furnace room of the old rec center, converted into a theater in 1961. It seated 63 persons with barely any room for stage and actors. Yet many great productions were staged at this "theater in your lap" such as *Mr. Roberts*, pictured right.

Photo Courtesy of the Waterloo Community Playhouse

Baseball began in Waterloo as early as 1867 when there were six amateur teams in the city. In one early game, West Waterloo beat East 41-20. In 1904, the first professional team, the Waterloo Lulus, members of the Iowa State League, played in a ball park, back of what is now the Twin Torch Inn. In 1910, Waterloo was briefly part of the Three I League but was dumped after one year because of low attendance. Club names changed often. The team was known at different times as the Boosters, the Microbes, the Manufacturers, the Champs and the Hawks. Businesses often closed down the afternoon of home games to allow their workers to attend. In 1930, the games were played at a field near Electric Park on Westfield, one of the first in the nation with night lights. In 1937, the team, affiliated with the Cincinnati Reds, became known as the Red Hawks. A year later they were the White Hawks, a Chicago White Sox farm team. Since then, they have been affiliated with the Boston Red Sox, the Kansas City Royals and the Cleveland Indians. The present ball park, home of the Waterloo Indians, in Cedar River Park was built after the stadium on Westfield burned in 1942.

Photo Courtesy of the Waterloo Baseball Company

In 1969, the #1 fire station was moved from East Fifth Street (next to the East Library) to this modern building on Third and Franklin Streets. With a lounge, modern kitchen and air conditioning, the new station provides better living conditions for the firemen. In the work area, there is a hoist so that mechanics no longer need to work on the engines on their backs. This is the only station in downtown Waterloo. Other stations are located at Donald and Heath Streets, Ansborough and Headford, 617 Nevada and the corner of Highways 218 and 412. The #2 station at 1906 Randolph has been closed to allow some of the firemen to take paramedic training.

Photo Courtesy of Helen Hoy

The first St. Francis Hospital, when it was built on the corner of Independence and Idaho Streets, was known as Seraphic Heights Hospital. Its construction was funded by the Franciscan order of nuns with some help from the city. It was dedicated in 1912 but its 164 rooms and large chapel was not completely finished until 1916. In 1967, recognizing a need for a more up to date facility, the board voted to build the present St. Francis Hospital located on West Ninth. Black Hawk County purchased the old building on the east side for use as a county health center. People, who would ordinarily be sent to state schools such as Woodward, stay here to receive care in their own county.

Photo Courtesy of St. Francis Hospital

In 1969 Grant School became an alternative school known as the Bridgeway Project. The school was remodeled with classroom doors and walls removed and bright color schemes painted throughout the building. Students are organized into learning teams rather than grades. The tigers include children five years old to eight, the cougars, seven through ten, the ocelots, eight to eleven year-olds and the jaguars, nine to twelve. Each team possesses its own computer and computer literacy is taught from kindergarten on up. Enrollment in the school is voluntary with the student body population equally divided at 50% black and 50% white.

Photo Courtesy of the Waterloo Community Schools

The period of the seventies witnessed many changes on Fourth Street. Most of the stores pictured have either gone out of business or set up in shopping centers. Black's Building still stands, but no longer houses a department store. The Commercial Building across the street has been demolished as have the other buildings you see. The National Bank presently takes up part of the block and a small park, the remainder. Newer model buses still run but no longer on Fourth Street.

Photo Courtesy of Robert Levis

The show has changed in many ways. The word "Dairy" is no longer part of its name, and it is no longer a national dairy show. The Belgian horse show is discontinued but there is a draft horse show with all breeds exhibited. The swine and beef animal show remain two important events.

Photo Courtesy of the National Cattle Congress Fair

Another disaster struck the dairy show when the frame exhibition hall burned. It was replaced with this brick building called Estel Hall named after Edward Estel who held the job of dairy show manager longer than any of his predecessors. Not all the entertainment goes on in the hippodrome. A small crowd has gathered to watch young people perform.

Photo Courtesy of the National Cattle Congress Fair

Waterloo Savings Bank was the only bank in the city strong enough to withstand the brunt of the depression. Organized in 1903, for many years it was located on the corner of Fourth and Commercial next door to the Pioneer Bank. The Pioneer could not survive F.D.R.'s enforced bank holiday so Waterloo Savings took over the Pioneer's more impressive banking facility. In 1974 the bank moved to its present location on the west bank of the Cedar on Park Avenue.

Photo Courtesy of Helen Hoy

This aerial view of the National Cattle Congress grounds, taken in the early seventies, reveals how much the show has grown, now covering 86 acres. The hippodrome has been enlarged and has added a year-round heating and cooling system. Now called McElroy Auditorium, it is leased to the city of Waterloo and is the setting for numerous activities — ice hockey, basketball tournaments, rock shows and commencement exercises. The main gate is now on Rainbow Drive. Not much farm machinery is on exhibit as the pieces are too big and too expensive to move. Neither is much left of Electric Park. The IPS gas storage tank is gone. Across Westfield Avenue one can see the new John Deere Foundry. This is a good view of Sans Souci Island in the Cedar River.

Photo Courtesy of National Cattle Congress Fair

This "theme" park is situated on the banks of the Cedar River on Fletcher Avenue. Developed between 1963 and 1965, it is part of Hope Martin Park which provides picnic, fishing, and camping facilities. Many of the areas in the park are named after local Indians. "Whirling Thunder Trail" was named for a son of Chief Black Hawk, "Chief Little Priest Powwow Place" for another early Indian, and "Utolah's Wild Flower Garden" for an Indian maiden involved in a tragic romance with a white trapper.

Hope Martin Park is part of the Greenbelt which Leonard Katoski considers the park system's "treasure." The idea was first proposed in 1969 by Katoski; the mayor and council helped plan the financing. The Corps of Engineers and the Iowa Natural Resource Council set up a flood plain survey which helped establish the 800 acres of natural setting along Black Hawk Creek. The Federal government had the Open Spaces Agency which provided matching funds for the development of the Greenbelt. Today, hikers and naturalists can travel 22 miles of trail and enjoy the beauty of the woodland setting.
Photo Courtesy of Waterloo Park Commission

Tucked away in the Castle Hill area is one of Waterloo's ten theme parks. Called Ghost Town, it is a replica of an old west Main Street with false front buildings. Children are encouraged to climb around on these structures. There are even jail bars for little faces to peer out from.

Children can also visit another fantasy world at Cinderella Park near Central High School. The pumpkin coach is there as are six-foot tall white mice who seem to beckon children to climb on and perch behind their ears.
Photo Courtesy of Waterloo Park Commission

Ice hockey was played in Waterloo back in the late twenties and early thirties. The games took place in the unheated Dairy Cattle Show Hippodrome where the ice in the rink froze naturally. The depression and the mild winter of 1932 put a damper on that location. Today, the Waterloo Black Hawks play in McElroy Auditorium, the remodeled hippodrome. The building is heated comfortably for the fans and ice is artifically produced. The Black Hawks have been playing for Waterloo since 1962 and are the oldest established franchise in the United States Hockey League. They have latched on to the league and division championships several times. Other teams in their league include Austin, Bloomington, and St. Paul in Minnesota, Des Moines, Dubuque, Mason City and Sioux City, Iowa.
Photo Courtesy of the Waterloo Black Hawks

If you descend the lower level of the Grout Museum, you will discover how our pioneer ancestors lived. The exhibit displays a general store of a hundred years ago with its open cracker barrel, coffee mill, lanterns, cheese and household goods. The far left end of the counter has an old-time drug store. This level also houses a pioneer cabin such as the Mullans or Hannas might have lived in, as well as antique farm implements and a blacksmith shop. There are also models of hoopskirted women and Victorian furniture. Several cases are devoted to the history of lighting and lamps, one of which displays railroad memorabilia. Displays are changed frequently. The Grout Museum features speakers, expert in different areas relating to local history. The Northeast Iowa Genealogical Society and the Cedar Valley Historical Society are two organizations who call the museum home.

Photo Courtesy of Grout Museum of History and Science

Opened in 1972, Central High is the most recently built school to date. At a cost of 4.3 million dollars, the facility is air conditioned and features classrooms with moveable walls and a driver training range. School populations, on the wane, necessitated the closing of 10 schools in the following decade. Hawthorne became an alternative school, Nellie Garvey, a teacher information center and Lafayette, for a time, was used by Hawkeye Institute of Technology. In 1982, the district decided on a new plan to transform all schools in the Waterloo system. The high schools became four year schools. McKinstry Junior High, an elementary school, and the remaining junior high schools were turned into middle schools with grades 6-8. The elementary schools had grades kindergarten through fifth.

Photo Courtesy of the Waterloo Community Schools

The new YMCA on the corner of South Hackett Road and University Avenue emphasizes physical activities for the entire family. Beyond the spacious lobby, members can enjoy a large lounge and game room. Classes are offered in aquatics, karate, judo, racquetball, golf, gymnastics or aerobic exercise. Facilities include an Olympic swimming pool, small pool, running track, weight room, exercise room and a babysitting service is available. Family Sundays are set aside from November 26 to March to give opportunity for families to use the facilities together.

Photo Courtesy of Black Hawk County YMCA

Waterloo's first YWCA materialized in 1884 when three college girls, Winnie Fisk, Belle Ayers and Carrie Rutledge formed a group and rented rooms on the second floor of 181 West Fourth Street. Sunday vesper services, social events for girls and mixed groups, and afternoon teas for women made up the program. In 1887, that building was sold and it was not until 1889 that space was rented at 510 Commercial Street. New classes included etiquette and the teaching of English to immigrant women. Lack of funds caused the "Y" to close in 1893. In 1911, renewed interest and an effective membership campaign brought in 2000 members and over 3,000 dollars. New quarters were rented at 611 Sycamore. In 1913, they moved to the second floor of a building in the 100 block of East Fourth Street. Here the "Y" ran a cafeteria where one could get a meal for about 20 cents. A building fund was started. The first contributor was Miss Frances Grout, who gave her home on Third Street to the project. In 1919, the building fund received a sizable legacy from the estate of C. J. Fowler. In 1922, the present property was purchased from St. Mary's Church. Mortimer Cleveland was the architect selected to design the building. In 1924, the new YWCA opened its doors and has continued to serve Waterloo in this location ever since.

Photo Courtesy of the YWCA

Nutritious meals are an important part of the Hawkeye Valley Agency's services to the elderly. The nutrition center at SAC's is one of 18 in a ten county area and one of two in Waterloo. The second is located at the senior Center at the Jesse Cosby Center on Mobile Street.
Photo Courtesy of SAC's on Seventh

Allen Memorial Hospital was the gift of a Waterloo lawyer, H.B. Allen, who came to the young town in 1857. He married the daughter of Hardin Nowlin who had served in the territorial legislature. The hospital is a memorial to his wife. Mr. Allen provided not only the money for the original building but also 15 acres from a family farm as a site. The first part of the hospital was built in 1921 and it has been added to several times. Today, the hospital provides four educational services: a school for nurses, training for radiological and medical technicians, and clinical pastoral education. Open heart surgery and CT scanning are performed here. There is a psychiatric unit, a regional poison information center and the hospital provides a telephone information service on medical problems.
Photo Courtesy of the Allen Memorial Hospital

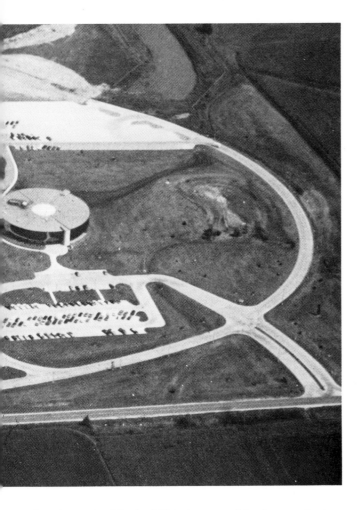

When Hawkeye Institute of Technology first opened in 1966, it opened doors all over town with its programs being taught in many different locations. Gradually, all classes have been brought together at the school's new campus on East Orange Road, south of the Crossroads Shopping Center. After 1983, there will be only one program taught off campus, Adult Basic Education located at 844 West Fourth Street. Since it opened, over 12,000 students have taken advantage of the vocational and technical courses offered. Enrollment of full-time students runs around 2,000. The institute offers 45 career programs varying from one month to eight quarters in length. Students can select courses ranging from aviation technology and farming to police training.

Photo Courtesy of the Hawkeye Institute of Technology

When the National Bank of Waterloo opened its doors on June 15, 1933 at 10 A.M., fireworks went off and 16 planes flew in formation over the downtown area. The opening of a new bank was something to celebrate as three of Waterloo's four banks had folded after the bank holiday of 1932. With assets from the defunct Commercial Bank and help from the Reconstruction Finance Corporation, the new bank began doing business at the site of the former First National Bank at Sycamore and Fourth Streets. In 1953, the bank purchased the Black's Grocery Store on Park Avenue and moved there. In 1976, they moved to their present building (opposite page), architecturally one of the most striking in the city. The old bank was demolished to make room for parking. The drive-up banking facility is two blocks east on Park Avenue. There are branch banks at Crossroads Shopping Center, Ridgeway Plaza and Logan Plaza.

Photo Courtesy of Helen Hoy

Dan Gable, "the greatest pinner in college history", was the winner of 180 consecutive high school and college wrestling matches. He competed in the Olympics without a point scored against him and is distinguished as the first American to win back-to-back world championships. He attended West High School where his record was 64-0. In his junior year at Iowa State University in Ames, he received the "Outstanding Wrestler Award." He took top honors at the Pan American games and, at the Tbilisi tournament in Russia, he was also recognized as "Outstanding Wrestler". Presently he coaches wrestling at the University of Iowa.

Photo Courtesy of Robert Siddens

In June of 1982 and again in 1983, the Waterloo Chamber of Commerce and the Waterloo Downtown Council sponsored Waterloo Days, a week of celebration - parades, shows, tournaments - which may become an annual tradition. Many businesses, Rath's, the hospitals, the *Courier*, Banco Mortgage, held open house and gave tours. Rath's served free wieners to picnickers in Cedar River Park. The festival also featured balloon ascensions, flower shows, and an ethnic food festival in Lincoln Park.

Photo Courtesy of the Waterloo Chamber of Commerce

The First Federal Savings Bank in the remodeled Strand theater building lays claim to the oldest financial institution in the city. In 1878, a group of Waterloo businessmen organized the Waterloo Building and Loan Company with the Honorable Matt Parrott as president. The first office was in the Marsh Place Building and the company had offices in different locations in the east business district. In 1955, the bank raised a new building next to the Strand Theater. When the Strand went out of business, the Waterloo Savings and Loan took over the theater and turned it into a modern banking facility. In July, 1983, they became First Federal Savings Bank.

Photo Courtesy of Helen Hoy

A remodeled A&P grocery store provides the site for SAC's on Seventh, a senior citizen activity center. Sponsored by the Hawkeye Valley Area Agency on Aging, it is located at 415 East Seventh Street. All services are provided on a contribution basis to persons 60 years or older and their spouses, regardless of social or economic means. Here, older people are welcomed for meals, card playing or crafts. The first senior activity center was located on Fifth Street in an old Bishop's cafeteria. It provided social activities but lacked facilities for meal service.

Photo Courtesy of Hawkeye Valley Area Agency on Aging

Moving to the Hope Martin Theater in the new recreation center was an exciting change for the Waterloo Playhouse. The new theater accommodated 343 playgoers and its wide stage allowed for more than a suggestion of scenery. In 1970, the season ticket holders numbered 1,100 and the yearly attendance was at 8,000. By 1982, there were 6,000 season ticket holders with over 46,000 attending. The annual budget is more than $250,000. The staff has grown from one man in 1970 to 8 full-time plus part-timers. In 1982, the playhouse merged with the Black Hawk Children's Theater. Along with the children's theater, the playhouse produces 14 shows per season. In 1983, the organization received the Iowa Award for distinguished service to the arts. The scene in the photo is from *My Fair Lady*, one of the most popular plays ever produced by the WCP.

Photo Courtesy of the Waterloo Community Playhouse

In the early part of this century, Waterloo had 12 banking institutions. As a result of the depression, there were only two banks left operating in the city. In 1943, George Albee organized the Peoples Savings Bank which opened for business with three officers and five staff members in the old Black Hawk Bank Building. By 1960, the staff had augmented to seven officers and 43 employees. Growth demanded a new facility and the bank moved to a new building at 419 West Fourth Street. Twenty years later, the decision was made to retain the same site but completely remodel the building, filling the need for additional space. The new facade is eyecatching, unusual and appealing.
Photo Courtesy of Helen Hoy

The Gates Golf Course is located in the city's largest park, 237-acre Gates Park. In the late 1920s, the Park Board authorized construction of a 9-hole sand green golf course at Gates Park on Waterloo's east side at Donald Street. Another 9 holes were added in the mid-50s and the sand greens changed to grass.

Construction of a third municipal golf course started in 1968 on the extreme south edge of Waterloo, approximately 1 1/2 miles south of Crossroads. South Hills is self-supporting although not as popular as the other courses. Gates Park is also home of the city's first municipal swimming pool, built in 1960 and replaced in 1980.
Photo Courtesy of the Waterloo Park Commission

Conway Civic Center has a unique name and purpose. Conway means "connecting way" between east and west Waterloo and exemplifies people caring for their total community. The impetus for a civic center started in the early 1970s. Cedar Skyline Corporation began promoting the concept in 1972. Mayor Lloyd Turner, the city council and the Waterloo Industrial Development Association took over in 1973. The purchase of the land and demolition of the buildings were completed in 1974. The citizens of Waterloo had passed a general obligation bond in 1973 for 4.5 million dollars. Final cost of the project was 4.91 million. Conway was opened in September, 1975, without the hotel and parking lot that were part of the original design. This phase was completed in 1983 when a Holiday Inn with a connecting skyway to the civic center was constructed. The center, with 36,000 square feet of convention hall space, has been used for a variety of activities from large conventions lasting several days to single day events.
Photo Courtesy of the Holiday Inn

Schoitz Medical Center on Kimball and Ridgeway is the successor to the old Presbyterian hospital formerly located on Leavitt Street. It was built in 1951 and named in honor of Charlotte Lee Schoitz, wife of Otto, a major funder. In 1982, the name was changed to Schoitz Medical Center. It has been enlarged and remodeled several times, most recently in 1982 when the adjoining Medical Arts Building for doctors' offices was completed. Some of the services offered include nuclear medical services, substance abuse treatment, young family health program, rehabilitation program for spinal cord and brain injuries, CT scanning and full time emergency room physician. The hospital also serves as a regional trauma center. West High School is in the background.

Photo Courtesy of Schoitz Medical Center

Crossroads Shopping Center, with complete climate control and acres of parking, was built in 1970 at the junction of 218 south and highway 412. The Sears and J.C. Penney stores were the first retail businesses to move from downtown Waterloo onto the mall. There are 67 businesses presently located in the building and 13 on the perimeter. There are two levels reached by either stairs or escalators. A large concourse in the center of the building provides an area for craft sales, antique shows or special events. Many senior citizens and those suffering heart ailments find the enclosed space to be an excellent walking concourse.

Photo Courtesy of Crossroads Shopping Center

The Waterloo-Cedar Falls Symphony also calls the Recreation Center home. They have an office located in the complex and use the rehearsal halls. The symphony gives twelve concerts a year presented in the West High School auditorium, half of which include a performance by an outstanding guest soloist.
Photo Courtesy of the Waterloo Recreation Commission

Recognized as the city's oldest business, the *Waterloo Courier* has, over a span of 114 years, been published from 11 different locations, all on the west side and pivoting within a few blocks of its present modern facility on Park and Commercial. In its long and progressive life, it has absorbed all competition: *The Reporter* published by the Matt Parrott Company, the *Times Tribune* formerly owned by the Tribune Press and more recently, the *Cedar Falls Record*. When Montgomery Ward moved their store to College Square Shopping Mall, the *Courier* purchased the building and moved its presses onto the first floor. The *Courier,* founded by W. H. Hartman in 1859, was owned by the W. H. Hartman Company until 1983 when it was bought by Howard Publications of California.
Photo Courtesy of Helen Hoy

The original recreation center was located in the abandoned Washington School on East Fourth Street. Ray Forsberg, director from 1952 to 1978, had a philosophy that it was the community's responsibility to provide for the artistic and cultural development of its citizens. The Washington facility was closed in 1964 and for a time the recreation center was housed in the Hawkeye Tech Building on Commercial Street. The new Recreation Center on the west bank of the Cedar was opened in 1966, containing the Hope Martin Theater, Lichty and Rotary Galleries, administrative offices, several multi-purpose rooms, rehearsal halls for the Waterloo Symphony and the playhouse. The complex was privately funded with only a small amount of tax money used. The center became more and more popular creating a demand for further expansion. In 1978, the privately funded arts and crafts wing was opened. The surrounding land was relandscaped and the Rath fountain added. The center employs 18 administrative personnel plus support and maintenance crew.

Photo Courtesy of the Waterloo Recreation Center

The center has several galleries for the display of paintings and sculpture. The Raymond Forsberg Riverside Gallery (photo) in the new wing, displays travelling art shows or special exhibits of works by well-known artists. The center also possesses its own permanent collection of paintings and sculpture.

Photo Courtesy of the Waterloo Recreation Commission

Ballet is only one of the many dance classes available for both children and adults at the Recreation Center. Painting, pottery throwing, photography or bridge are also offered. The Recreation Center's sports program includes a wide variety of classes ranging from skiing and skating to rowing. A midwest regatta has become a recent annual affair. The sports department is also responsible for an eight week summertime, playground program as well as a cultural exploration series. The center's Junior Art Gallery annually creates a special theme show. The 1983-84 theme centers on Native Americans.

Photo Courtesy of the Waterloo Recreation Commission

At the north and south walls of the main area in the new Public Library are two examples of the kind of murals which appeared in many public buildings in the depression years. Part of the cost of Federal buildings could be used for either sculpture or paintings, so when this structure was planned as a post office in 1938, Edgar Britton was chosen to create two murals. Britton was a product of the midwest. Born in Nebraska in 1901, he had grown up in Iowa. He went to the University of Iowa to study dentistry but soon dropped out to pursue a career in art. He studied with Grant Wood, collaborating on murals. Before receiving his commission to do the murals for the Waterloo Post Office, he had worked on a number of PWA and WPA projects. He was technical director for the WPA federal arts project. He had done frescoes for several public buildings in Illinois and for the Bureau of Mines building in Washington, D.C. His paintings are among 50 commissioned for public buildings in Iowa in the depression years and are representative of midwest regional art of the thirties. Not everyone liked his portrayal of Iowans. Some thought his stocky figures suggested European peasants. The mural entitled "Exposition" did not convey the scope of Dairy Cattle Congress. When the post office was in the process of being remodeled into the library, there was some question whether the paintings could be preserved. They have been preserved and patrons of the library seem to enjoy them more as part of the library decor than they ever did in the post office.

Photo Courtesy of Helen Hoy

In 1981, when the Waterloo post office moved to a new location on Sycamore Street, it left a large building which was creatively transformed into a beautiful, spacious and efficient library. The old Carnegie libraries had long been too small for the size of the collection and the amount of service offered. Changing a federal building into a modern library took a lot of remodeling. The photo shows the wing added at the rear which accommodates the bookmobile and adds more floor space for the nonfiction collection on the second floor. Automatic doors were installed at the main entrance and a ramp for the handicapped constructed. New plantings of shrubs and trees enhance the library's exterior. Before remodeling began, pieces of marble, doors, fixtures, plumbing were removed. Through an auction of these items, the Friends of the Library made $12,000 to be used for new library equipment.

Photo Courtesy of Waterloo Public Library

An impressive stairway (or the elevator) moves patrons from the first floor to the second. Beyond the stairwell is the children's department, guarded by a large green dragon. The first floor level houses the check out desk, audiovisual department, meeting rooms and the fiction collection. The second floor locates nonfiction books, magazines, newspapers, reference desk, microfilms, readers and main card catalogue. The library is in the process of computerizing the catalog. There are study rooms, some with typewriters, for those who seek a quiet place to work. The overall decor is in pleasant earth tones that make for a restful atmosphere. Comfortable chairs in contrasting bright colors highlight the decor on both levels.

Photo Courtesy of the Waterloo Public Library

Acknowledgements

In compiling this publication, in-depth historical explanations were, by necessity, limited. Each subject covered deserves further study and we encourage readers to continue this valuable research.

Material for this book was gleaned from personal and recorded interviews, newspaper files and past publications. Every effort was made to be accurate yet further research may clarify and revise present information or reveal new sources.

Our special thanks to these individuals without whose help this book could never have been published: Mike Phipps, former director of the Waterloo Public Library and the library staff, Don Durchenwald, Leonard Katoski, Helen and Jean Klinefelter, Robert Levis, Barb Gregersen and the staff of the Grout Museum of History and Science.

Others who contributed include Fred Adams, Marshall Adesman, Clarence Alling, Clarence Baldwin, Dorothy Bondurant, Virgil Clark, Orville Close, Reed Craft, Melba Durchenwald, Ross Galloway, Vera Howard, Sharon Juan, Marion Lichty, Roseann Mathews, Gene Meeker, Dean Myhr, George Patty, Sue Pearson, Randy Pilkington, James Redden, Sol Serber, Georgianna Stewart, Lloyd Turner, Hamilton Weidner, Deere and Company, Rath Packing Company, Dart Truck Company.

Bibliography

Allen, Birney. *Glimpses of Waterloo*, 1905.

Atlas of Black Hawk County, Iowa Publishling Company, 1910.

Atlas of Iowa, Andreas.

Baldwin, Clarence. *Crossroads on the Cedar*, 1967.

Baldwin, Clarence. *Historical Sketches*, 1982.

Citizens Gas and Electric Company. *Waterloo Way Wins: A Souvenir*, 1910.

Hartman, John. *History of Black Hawk County*, 1915.

History of Black Hawk County, Western Publishing Company, 1878.

Leavitt, Roger. When Waterloo Was Young, address to the Waterloo Rotary Club, 1929.

Maravetz, Steve. Love Affair with the Bush Leagues, unpublished manuscript.

Means, O. M. *Waterloo: A Fin de Siecle Sketch*, 1898.

Palimpsest, February 1959, August, 1972.

Pictorial Review of West Waterloo Schools, 1933-34.

Robinson, Charles. *The Well-being of Waterloo*, Civic Society, 1910.

Town Criers Club, Waterloo. *The Tale of an Hundred Smoke Stacks*, 1912.

Van Metre, Isaiah. *History of Black Hawk County*, 1904.

Waterloo Courier. Centennial Edition, 1854-1954, June 20, 1954.

Waterloo. Author and publisher unknown, ca. 1910.

Weston, Gynne, F. for the Chamber of Commerce n.d. (ca. 1928) *The Story of Waterloo: The Factory City of Iowa*.

INDEX